ALKALINE NUTRITION COOKBOOK

TABLE OF CONTENTS

CHAPTER 1

UNDERSTANDING ALKALINE NUTRITION

- **What is Alkaline Nutrition?**

Alkaline Nutrition, often referred to as an alkaline diet, is a dietary approach that emphasizes the consumption of foods that have an alkaline or basic effect on the body's pH (potential of hydrogen) levels. In the context of this nutritional philosophy, pH values below 7 are considered acidic, while values above 7 are deemed alkaline or basic.

The central idea behind Alkaline Nutrition is to maintain the body's pH level slightly on the alkaline side, which proponents claim may offer various health benefits. This approach is rooted in the belief that an overly acidic internal environment can potentially contribute to health issues and that consuming alkaline foods can help restore balance.

Alkaline foods primarily consist of fruits, vegetables, nuts, seeds, and legumes. These foods are typically rich in essential vitamins, minerals, and antioxidants. They are thought to have an alkalinizing effect on the body when metabolized, helping to counteract the acidity that can result from a diet high in processed foods, meat, dairy, and other acidic choices.

Some commonly consumed alkaline foods include:

- Leafy greens: Spinach, kale, and Swiss chard.

- Citrus fruits: Lemons, limes, and oranges.

- Root vegetables: Sweet potatoes and carrots.

- Nuts and seeds: Almonds, flaxseeds, and chia seeds.

- Legumes: Lentils and chickpeas.

It's important to note that Alkaline Nutrition is often criticized for lacking robust scientific evidence to support many of its claims. While proponents argue that it can help improve overall health and well-being, including by reducing the risk of chronic diseases, more research is needed to fully understand its potential benefits.

Moreover, the human body has its mechanisms for regulating pH levels, primarily through the kidneys and lungs. These natural processes help maintain a stable internal pH, irrespective of the pH of the foods we consume. Nevertheless, the emphasis on a diet rich in alkaline foods can contribute to a well-rounded and nutrient-dense eating plan.

Individuals interested in adopting an alkaline diet should consult with healthcare professionals or registered dietitians to ensure it aligns with their specific health needs and goals. As with any dietary approach, balance and variety are key, and it's essential to consider overall nutritional requirements when making dietary choices.

- **The pH Scale: Acidic vs. Alkaline**

The pH scale is a measurement system used to determine the acidity or alkalinity of a substance. It quantifies the concentration of hydrogen ions (H+) in a solution, with values ranging from 0 to 14.

- **Acidic**: Solutions with a pH value less than 7 are considered acidic. The lower the pH, the more acidic the solution. For example, lemon juice and vinegar are acidic substances, with pH values below 3.

- **Neutral**: A pH of 7 is considered neutral. Pure water is a common example of a neutral substance, with an equal concentration of H+ and OH- ions.

- **Alkaline (or Basic)**: Solutions with a pH value greater than 7 are alkaline or basic. The higher the pH, the more alkaline the solution. Baking soda and soapy water are examples of alkaline substances, with pH values greater than 9.

The pH scale is logarithmic, which means that each whole number change on the scale represents a tenfold difference in acidity or alkalinity. For instance, a substance with a pH of 6 is ten times more acidic than a substance with a pH of 7, and a substance with a pH of 9 is ten times more alkaline than a substance with a pH of 8.

In the context of nutrition, the pH scale is often used to categorize foods and beverages as either acidic or alkaline. Some proponents of the alkaline diet suggest that consuming more alkaline foods can help balance the body's internal pH, potentially offering health benefits. However, it's important to note that the body has its mechanisms for regulating pH levels, and the impact of dietary pH on overall health is a topic of ongoing scientific research and debate.

- **Benefits of Alkaline Nutrition**

The potential benefits of Alkaline Nutrition, also known as the alkaline diet, have been a subject of discussion and research. While some proponents claim various health advantages, it's essential to recognize that the scientific evidence supporting these claims is still evolving, and more research is needed to make definitive conclusions. Here are some of the purported benefits associated with Alkaline Nutrition:

1. Improved Bone Health: Alkaline foods, such as leafy greens and certain fruits, are typically rich in minerals like calcium and magnesium. Proponents suggest that these minerals can help support bone health and reduce the risk of osteoporosis.

2. Reduced Risk of Chronic Diseases: The diet's emphasis on fruits and vegetables may provide essential antioxidants, vitamins, and phytonutrients. These components are believed to have potential protective effects against chronic diseases, including heart disease and certain cancers.

3. Enhanced Kidney Function: Alkaline Nutrition proponents claim that by reducing the dietary load of acid-forming foods, the kidneys can function more efficiently and reduce the risk of kidney stones and other kidney-related issues.

4. Improved Digestion: Alkaline foods are often high in dietary fiber, which can support healthy digestion and regular bowel movements. This may help prevent conditions like constipation.

5. Increased Energy and Vitality: Some individuals report feeling more energetic and vital when following an alkaline diet. This could be due to a reduction in processed foods and increased intake of nutrient-dense, natural foods.

6. Weight Management: Alkaline Nutrition advocates suggest that the diet may help with weight management by promoting a more balanced and healthful eating pattern.

7. Enhanced Immune Function: A diet rich in alkaline foods may provide essential nutrients to support the immune system and help the body defend against illnesses.

8. Alleviation of Acid Reflux: Some individuals with acid reflux symptoms may experience relief when following an alkaline diet, which reduces the intake of highly acidic foods.

It's important to approach these claimed benefits with caution and to consider the broader context. While an alkaline diet can provide a variety of healthful foods, it's not a guaranteed cure for all health concerns, and its effectiveness may vary from person to person. Also, the human body has its natural mechanisms for regulating pH levels, which can limit the impact of dietary pH on overall health.

Consulting with a healthcare professional or registered dietitian is recommended before making significant dietary changes, as individual dietary needs and health conditions can vary widely. Additionally, it's essential to maintain a balanced and varied diet that meets all nutritional requirements while considering specific health goals and concerns.

- **Alkaline Foods vs. Acidic Foods**

In the context of Alkaline Nutrition, foods are often categorized as either "alkaline" or "acidic" based on their potential impact on the body's pH levels. Here's a breakdown of alkaline foods versus acidic foods:

Alkaline Foods:

- Alkaline foods are those that are believed to have an alkalinizing effect on the body when metabolized. They tend to be rich in essential minerals like calcium, magnesium, and potassium.

- These foods are typically plant-based, including many fruits, vegetables, nuts, and seeds.

- Common alkaline foods include:

- Leafy greens (e.g., spinach, kale, chard)

- Fruits (e.g., lemons, watermelon, and avocados)

- Vegetables (e.g., broccoli, carrots, and cucumbers)

- Nuts and seeds (e.g., almonds, flaxseeds, and chia seeds)

- Legumes (e.g., lentils, chickpeas, and green peas)

Acidic Foods:

- Acidic foods are considered to have an acidifying effect on the body when metabolized. They are often associated with high levels of sulfur-containing amino acids and may increase the body's acid load.

- Many animal products, such as meat, dairy, and some grains, are classified as acidic.

- Common acidic foods include:

- Meat (e.g., beef, pork, and chicken)

- Dairy products (e.g., milk, cheese, and yogurt)

- Grains (e.g., wheat, oats, and rice)

- Processed foods (e.g., sugary snacks, sodas, and fried foods)

It's important to note that the categorization of foods as alkaline or acidic in Alkaline Nutrition is based on the potential acid or base-forming properties of these foods during metabolism. The concept of the alkaline diet suggests that reducing the consumption of acidic foods and increasing the intake of alkaline foods can help maintain a slightly alkaline pH in the body, potentially offering various health benefits.

However, it's essential to approach this dietary philosophy with some critical considerations:

1. **Body's Natural pH Regulation:** The human body has its natural mechanisms for regulating pH levels in the blood, which are highly effective. Dietary choices can influence urine pH but have a limited and temporary impact on the body's overall pH balance.

2. **Lack of Robust Scientific Evidence:** While the alkaline diet is based on sound nutritional principles, claims about its specific health benefits often lack strong scientific evidence. The diet's impact on overall health remains a topic of ongoing research and debate.

3. **Individual Variation:** People's dietary needs and health conditions can vary widely. What works for one person may not work for another, and it's important to consider individual circumstances and consult with healthcare professionals or registered dietitians for personalized advice.

In summary, the categorization of foods into alkaline and acidic groups is a fundamental concept in Alkaline Nutrition. However, its potential health benefits and long-term impact on the body's pH balance are areas of ongoing research and discussion within the field of nutrition.

- **The History of Alkaline Nutrition**

The history of Alkaline Nutrition, often referred to as the alkaline diet, is a journey that blends aspects of nutritional science, holistic health, and alternative medicine. While the modern concept of an alkaline diet gained popularity in recent decades, its roots can be traced back to ancient dietary philosophies and the pioneering work of health advocates.

Ancient Foundations:

- The concept of balancing acid and alkaline elements in one's diet can be traced to ancient civilizations. Traditional Chinese medicine and Ayurveda, the ancient system of medicine in India, both emphasized the importance of achieving harmony and balance within the body, including through dietary choices.

The pH Factor Emerges:

- The idea of dietary pH began to gain attention in the early 20th century. In the 1920s, biochemist Dr. Otto Warburg won a Nobel Prize for his research on the relationship between pH levels and cancer. This work contributed to the growing interest in pH balance within the body.

The Alkaline-Ash Hypothesis:

- In the mid-20th century, the alkaline-ash hypothesis emerged. This theory suggested that the mineral composition of foods, when metabolized, could affect the body's acid-base balance. It proposed that an alkaline diet, rich in fruits and vegetables, could help maintain a balanced pH.

Prominent Advocates:

- The alkaline diet gained notable attention through the work of proponents like Dr. Robert O. Young, whose books and teachings popularized the concept of maintaining an alkaline state in the body. His "pH Miracle" book series and other publications contributed to the diet's growing recognition.

Popularity in the 21st Century:

- Over the last few decades, the alkaline diet has gained prominence, with many individuals seeking to adopt this dietary approach as a means to improve overall health and well-being. The diet's emphasis on plant-based, nutrient-rich foods aligns with broader trends towards healthier eating.

Ongoing Research and Debate:

- While the alkaline diet has attracted attention and has a dedicated following, it has also faced criticism. Some of the claims made by proponents lack robust scientific evidence, leading to ongoing debates within the scientific and nutrition communities.

In summary, the history of Alkaline Nutrition is a combination of ancient wisdom and modern understanding of nutrition and pH balance. Its emergence as a popular dietary philosophy reflects a broader interest in holistic health and the potential health benefits of consuming nutrient-dense, plant-based foods. As research in the field of nutrition continues, the impact and scientific validity of the alkaline diet on overall health will remain a subject of investigation and discussion.

CHAPTER 2

THE SCIENCE BEHIND ALKALINE NUTRITION

- **How the Body Maintains pH Balance**

The human body tightly regulates its pH balance to ensure optimal physiological function and maintain a stable internal environment. This balance is essential because even slight deviations in pH can have profound effects on biochemical processes. Here's how the body maintains pH balance:

1. **Buffers in Body Fluids:** The body uses a system of buffers to resist changes in pH. Buffers are substances, such as bicarbonate ions (HCO_3^-) and phosphate ions (HPO_4^{2-}), that can absorb excess H^+ ions to prevent pH changes. The bicarbonate buffer system in the blood is especially important in maintaining a stable pH.

2. **Respiratory Regulation:** The lungs play a critical role in pH regulation by controlling the concentration of carbon dioxide (CO_2) in the blood. When CO_2 levels increase, it combines with water to form carbonic acid (H_2CO_3), which releases H^+ ions and lowers pH. The lungs can expel excess CO_2 through increased ventilation, reducing the concentration of H^+ ions and raising pH. Conversely, slower breathing can retain CO_2 and decrease pH.

3. **Renal Regulation:** The kidneys have a profound influence on pH balance. They filter the blood and excrete excess H+ ions and reabsorb bicarbonate ions to help regulate pH. Additionally, the kidneys can synthesize new bicarbonate ions when needed and excrete excess H+ ions as ammonium (NH4+).

4. **Acid-Base Homeostasis:** The body maintains a delicate balance between acid-forming and base-forming processes. Many metabolic reactions produce acids as byproducts, such as carbonic acid (H2CO3) from aerobic metabolism. However, these acids are balanced by alkaline substances formed during metabolism and excreted in urine or eliminated through respiration.

5. **Hormonal Regulation:** Hormones like aldosterone and parathyroid hormone play roles in pH regulation. Aldosterone helps maintain electrolyte balance in the kidneys, which indirectly affects pH. Parathyroid hormone influences calcium and phosphate levels, which can impact pH regulation.

6. **Dietary Factors:** The body's pH balance is influenced by dietary choices. However, the impact of diet on overall pH is relatively limited, as the body has strong regulatory mechanisms. The kidneys can excrete excess acid or base in response to dietary intake to maintain pH within a narrow range.

7. **Urinary Excretion:** The kidneys filter the blood and excrete excess H+ ions into the urine. They also reabsorb bicarbonate ions and release ammonium ions to help maintain pH balance.

8. **Adaptive Responses:** The body can adapt to long-term pH changes by altering the rate of excretion of H+ ions or the reabsorption of bicarbonate ions in the kidneys, allowing it to maintain pH within the normal range.

In summary, the body employs a sophisticated and interconnected system of buffers, respiratory adjustments, renal regulation, and hormonal responses to maintain pH balance. This ensures that the body's pH remains within a narrow range, typically around 7.thirty five to 7.forty five in the blood, allowing for the proper functioning of enzymes and physiological processes.

- **Alkaline Minerals: Calcium, Magnesium, and Potassium**

Alkaline minerals, including calcium, magnesium, and potassium, play vital roles in maintaining the body's acid-base balance and overall health. These minerals are considered alkaline because they contribute to an alkaline or basic environment in the body when metabolized. Here's an overview of their functions:

Calcium:

- **Function:** Calcium is one of the most abundant minerals in the body, and it serves various crucial functions. In addition to its role in maintaining strong bones and teeth, calcium is involved in muscle contractions, including the beating of the heart, and plays a part in nerve transmission. Furthermore, it is essential for blood clotting, and it contributes to the activation of numerous enzymes involved in various metabolic processes.

- **Alkaline Effect:** When calcium is metabolized, it contributes to the neutralization of excess hydrogen ions (H+) in the body, effectively raising the pH level. By acting as a buffer, it helps maintain the acid-base balance in bodily fluids, which is essential for overall health.

- **Food Sources:** Calcium is found in a variety of foods, with dairy products being some of the most well-known sources. Milk, cheese, and yogurt are rich in calcium. However, for individuals who are lactose intolerant or follow a dairy-free diet, other sources include fortified plant-based milks (e.g., almond milk, soy milk), leafy green vegetables (e.g., kale, broccoli), almonds, sesame seeds, and sardines with bones.

Magnesium:

- **Function:** Magnesium is a versatile mineral involved in numerous enzymatic reactions in the body. It is essential for muscle function, including the relaxation of muscles, and it plays a vital role in nerve transmission. Magnesium is crucial for maintaining heart rhythm and blood pressure and is involved in energy metabolism. It also supports bone health.

- **Alkaline Effect:** Similar to calcium, magnesium has an alkaline effect as it helps buffer excess acidity, aiding in the body's maintenance of a balanced pH.

- **Food Sources:** Good dietary sources of magnesium include green leafy vegetables (e.g., spinach, Swiss chard, and collard greens), nuts (e.g., almonds, cashews), seeds (e.g., pumpkin seeds, sunflower seeds), whole grains (e.g., brown rice, quinoa), and legumes (e.g., black beans, lentils).

Potassium:

- **Function:** Potassium is an essential mineral for maintaining fluid balance within cells and tissues. It is vital for proper muscle contractions, including those of the heart muscle. Potassium helps regulate nerve impulses, making it essential for normal neurological function. Furthermore, it plays a significant role in managing blood pressure and heart rhythm.

- **Alkaline Effect:** Potassium contributes to the body's alkaline state by helping to counteract excessive acidity, thus supporting the body's acid-base balance.

- **Food Sources:** Potassium-rich foods are abundant and include bananas, oranges, citrus fruits, potatoes, sweet potatoes, leafy greens (e.g., spinach and Swiss chard), and beans (e.g., black beans, kidney beans). Consuming a diet rich in these foods can provide an adequate intake of potassium, which is important for overall health.

While these alkaline minerals are important for maintaining pH balance in the body, it's worth noting that they play a much broader role in various physiological processes. A well-balanced diet that includes a variety of nutrient-rich foods is essential to ensure you get adequate amounts of these minerals and other vital nutrients. Additionally, individual dietary needs may vary, so consulting with a healthcare professional or registered dietitian is advisable for personalized dietary recommendations.

- **Acidic Waste Products and Detoxification**

The body produces acidic waste products as a natural part of metabolism, and it has effective mechanisms for detoxification to maintain its internal environment within a narrow pH range. Here, we'll delve into the creation of acidic waste products, the body's detoxification processes, and how they collectively contribute to maintaining overall health.

Production of Acidic Waste Products:

- Metabolic processes in the body, such as the breakdown of carbohydrates, proteins, and fats, naturally generate acidic byproducts. For example, the metabolism of glucose produces carbon dioxide, which combines with water to form carbonic acid (H_2CO_3). Similarly, the breakdown of amino acids results in the production of sulfuric and phosphoric acids. These acidic compounds release hydrogen ions (H^+), contributing to acidity in the body's fluids.

Detoxification and pH Regulation:

- The body has several mechanisms to manage and neutralize these acidic waste products and maintain pH balance:

- **Respiratory System:** The lungs play a key role in regulating blood pH by controlling the elimination of carbon dioxide (CO_2). When CO_2 levels increase, it combines with water to form carbonic acid, which releases H^+ ions and lowers pH. Increased ventilation, such as during deep breathing, expels excess CO_2 and raises pH.

- **Renal System:** The kidneys are vital for pH regulation. They filter the blood and excrete excess H^+ ions into the urine. Additionally, they reabsorb bicarbonate ions (HCO_3^-) and release ammonium (NH_4^+) ions to help maintain a balanced pH.

- **Buffering Systems:** The body employs buffering systems to resist pH changes. These systems involve substances like bicarbonate ions (HCO_3^-) and phosphate ions (HPO_4^{2-}), which can absorb excess H^+ ions and neutralize acidity.

- **Diet and Nutrition:** The consumption of alkaline-forming foods, primarily fruits and vegetables, helps counteract the accumulation of acidic waste products. These foods provide bicarbonate ions and other alkaline substances to aid in pH balance.

Detoxification and Health:

- While the term "detoxification" is often used in the context of health and wellness, it's essential to clarify that the body's natural detoxification processes are ongoing and do not necessarily require special diets or detox programs. The body is equipped to manage the elimination of waste products efficiently.

- A balanced diet rich in nutrient-dense foods, especially fruits and vegetables, can support the body's detoxification and pH-regulating processes. These foods provide antioxidants and phytonutrients that help protect cells and tissues from oxidative damage.

- Detoxification is an essential aspect of overall health, as it enables the body to rid itself of waste products and maintain a healthy internal environment. However, the idea of "detox diets" or extreme fasting should be approached with caution, as these can potentially disrupt the body's natural detoxification processes and may lack scientific support.

In summary, the body's natural detoxification and pH regulation processes are integral to maintaining overall health. Adequate hydration, a balanced diet rich in fruits and vegetables, and regular physical activity are key factors in supporting the body's natural detoxification mechanisms and sustaining pH balance within a narrow and healthy range.

- **Alkaline Diet and Chronic Diseases**

The alkaline diet has been the subject of interest in relation to chronic diseases, with proponents suggesting that it may help prevent or alleviate certain health conditions. However, it's important to note that while the diet's principles align with sound nutritional practices, claims about its specific impact on chronic diseases often lack strong scientific evidence. Here is an overview of the relationship between the alkaline diet and chronic diseases:

1. Osteoporosis:

- **The Claim:** The alkaline diet is often associated with a reduced risk of osteoporosis. Proponents argue that the diet's emphasis on alkaline foods like leafy greens and certain fruits can help maintain bone health by reducing the need for the body to leach calcium from bones to neutralize excess acidity.

- **The Reality:** Calcium is essential for bone health, but the diet's impact on osteoporosis remains a topic of ongoing research and debate. While some studies suggest that a diet rich in fruits and vegetables may be associated with better bone health, the link between the alkaline diet and osteoporosis prevention is not well-established.

2. Heart Disease:

- **The Claim:** Supporters of the alkaline diet suggest that it can help reduce the risk of heart disease. The diet's focus on plant-based, low-sodium, and low-sugar foods may contribute to better cardiovascular health.

- **The Reality:** An emphasis on fruits and vegetables, as promoted by the alkaline diet, aligns with heart-healthy dietary recommendations. A diet high in these foods can help lower the risk of heart disease by reducing blood pressure and cholesterol levels. However, it's essential to maintain a balanced diet and lifestyle to address all risk factors for heart disease.

3. Diabetes:

- **The Claim:** Some proponents of the alkaline diet argue that it can help manage blood sugar levels, potentially reducing the risk of type two diabetes.

- **The Reality:** The alkaline diet's focus on low-glycemic index foods (e.g., whole grains, fruits, and vegetables) can be beneficial for individuals with diabetes or those at risk. However, more research is needed to establish a direct link between the alkaline diet and diabetes prevention or management.

4. Cancer:

- **The Claim:** There are claims that an alkaline diet can reduce the risk of cancer by creating an inhospitable environment for cancer cells, which are believed to thrive in an acidic environment.

- **The Reality:** The relationship between diet and cancer is complex, and no single dietary approach has been proven to prevent or cure cancer. While a diet rich in fruits and vegetables may offer some protective effects against certain types of cancer, it is not a guaranteed prevention strategy.

5. Inflammation:

- **The Claim:** Alkaline foods are often associated with reduced inflammation, which plays a role in chronic diseases.

- **The Reality:** An anti-inflammatory diet is characterized by the consumption of foods like fruits and vegetables, which are also staples of the alkaline diet. Reducing chronic inflammation is associated with a lower risk of chronic diseases.

In conclusion, the alkaline diet's focus on nutrient-dense, plant-based foods aligns with several principles of a healthy diet that can help reduce the risk of chronic diseases. However, claims about its specific impact on chronic diseases should be approached with caution, as more research is needed to establish direct links between the alkaline diet and disease prevention or management. It is advisable to maintain a balanced diet and consult with healthcare professionals for personalized guidance on managing chronic diseases.

- **Research and Studies on Alkaline Nutrition**

Research and studies on alkaline nutrition, often referred to as the alkaline diet, have garnered attention in recent years. However, it's important to note that the scientific evidence supporting the claims and benefits of the alkaline diet remains somewhat limited and is a subject of ongoing investigation and debate. Here's an overview of the research and studies conducted on alkaline nutrition:

1. Acid-Base Balance and Diet:

- Numerous studies have explored the relationship between diet and the body's acid-base balance. These studies have investigated the effects of various dietary patterns on pH levels in the body. While they provide valuable insights into the impact of diet on acidity, there is no consensus on the specific pH levels that are most beneficial for health.

2. Bone Health:

- Some research has examined the potential influence of an alkaline diet on bone health. This research suggests that diets high in alkaline-forming foods, such as fruits and vegetables, may have a positive impact on bone density. However, the specific mechanisms and long-term effects are still areas of ongoing research.

3. Muscle Performance:

- Studies have investigated the impact of dietary acid-base balance on muscle performance, particularly during high-intensity exercise. Some research suggests that acid-forming diets may lead to muscle fatigue and decreased exercise performance. This has led to discussions about the potential benefits of an alkaline diet for athletes and physically active individuals.

4. Urinary pH and Diet:

- Research has explored the relationship between dietary choices and urinary pH levels. These studies have found that diet can influence urine pH, with diets rich in alkaline-forming foods resulting in more alkaline urine. However, the implications of urine pH on overall health remain a topic of debate.

5. Chronic Disease Risk:

- Some studies have examined the association between dietary patterns, including alkaline diets, and the risk of chronic diseases. Research suggests that diets rich in fruits and vegetables, which are central to the alkaline diet, may be associated with a reduced risk of certain chronic diseases. However, more research is needed to establish direct cause-and-effect relationships.

6. Weight Management:

- Research has investigated the potential effects of an alkaline diet on weight management. Some studies suggest that an alkaline diet may be associated with weight loss and improvements in body composition, but the mechanisms involved require further investigation.

7. Inflammation and Disease:

- Alkaline diets, which often emphasize anti-inflammatory foods, have been studied for their potential impact on inflammation and chronic diseases. Some research indicates that such diets may reduce markers of inflammation, but further studies are necessary to confirm these findings.

It's important to recognize that while there is research related to alkaline nutrition, the evidence supporting specific claims and benefits of the alkaline diet is not as robust as with other well-established dietary patterns. Scientific consensus regarding the impact of an alkaline diet on health is still evolving, and more high-quality, long-term studies are needed to provide conclusive evidence.

Individual dietary needs and health conditions can vary widely, so it's advisable to consult with healthcare professionals or registered dietitians for personalized dietary guidance and to make informed decisions about incorporating elements of the alkaline diet into one's overall eating pattern.

CHAPTER 3

SETTING THE FOUNDATION FOR AN ALKALINE LIFESTYLE

- **Assessing Your Current Diet**

Assessing your current diet is a crucial step in understanding your eating habits and making informed choices for your health and well-being. Here are some key steps and considerations to help you evaluate your diet:

1. Keep a Food Diary:

- Start by keeping a record of everything you eat and drink for at least a few days, ideally up to a week. Include the portion sizes and the time you consumed each meal or snack. Be as detailed as possible.

2. Analyze Macronutrient Intake:

- Review your food diary to assess your intake of macro**Nutrients:** carbohydrates, proteins, and fats. Consider whether your current intake aligns with your dietary goals and recommendations. For instance, are you getting an appropriate balance of these nutrients for your age, activity level, and health status?

3. Assess Micronutrient Intake:

- Evaluate your consumption of vitamins and minerals. Are you meeting your daily recommended intake of essential nutrients? Pay attention to specific nutrients that are important for your health, such as calcium, vitamin D, iron, and potassium.

4. Examine Food Quality:

- Consider the quality of the foods you consume. Are you eating whole, minimally processed foods like fruits, vegetables, whole grains, lean proteins, and healthy fats? Or is your diet primarily comprised of highly processed, sugary, and fatty foods?

5. Fiber Intake:

- Evaluate your fiber intake. Are you consuming enough fiber from whole grains, fruits, and vegetables? Adequate fiber intake is essential for digestive health and can help with weight management.

6. Hydration:

- Assess your daily fluid intake. Are you staying adequately hydrated by drinking enough water and other hydrating beverages? Dehydration can affect energy levels and overall well-being.

7. Dietary Patterns:

- Consider your dietary patterns. Are you following a particular eating plan, such as vegetarian, vegan, Mediterranean, or a low-carb diet? Assess whether your chosen dietary pattern aligns with your nutritional needs and health goals.

8. Meal Timing:

- Reflect on your eating schedule. Are you consuming meals and snacks at regular intervals throughout the day, or do you frequently skip meals or engage in erratic eating patterns? Consistency in meal timing can be beneficial for metabolism and appetite regulation.

9. Mindful Eating:

- Pay attention to your eating habits and behaviors. Are you practicing mindful eating, which involves savoring your food, eating without distractions, and recognizing hunger and fullness cues? Mindful eating can help prevent overeating and promote a healthier relationship with food.

10. Health Goals:

● Consider your health and dietary goals. Are you aiming to lose weight, manage a chronic condition, improve athletic performance, or simply maintain overall well-being? Your goals should guide your dietary choices.

11. Seek Professional Guidance:

● If you have specific dietary concerns, health conditions, or nutritional goals, it's advisable to consult with a healthcare professional or registered dietitian. They can provide personalized guidance and create a tailored dietary plan based on your needs.

By assessing your current diet, you can gain valuable insights into your eating habits and identify areas for improvement. Remember that making positive changes to your diet should be a gradual and sustainable process. Consult with healthcare professionals or registered dietitians for expert advice and support in achieving your dietary goals.

● **Transitioning to an Alkaline Diet**

Transitioning to an alkaline diet involves making intentional changes to your eating habits and choosing foods that are considered alkaline forming. Here are some steps to help you make a successful transition to an alkaline diet:

1. Educate Yourself:

● Begin by learning about alkaline-forming foods and their benefits. Understand the principles of the alkaline diet, including the concept of pH balance in the body.

2. Assess Your Current Diet:

● Evaluate your current eating habits by keeping a food diary, as mentioned earlier. This will help you identify areas where you can make changes and set specific goals for transitioning to an alkaline diet.

3. Gradual Transition:

● Transitioning to an alkaline diet doesn't have to be abrupt. It can be more manageable and sustainable if you make gradual changes over time. Start by incorporating more alkaline foods into your meals while reducing acidic foods.

4. Focus on Alkaline Foods:

- Prioritize alkaline-forming foods, such as fresh fruits, vegetables, nuts, seeds, and some whole grains. Aim to make these foods the foundation of your diet.

5. Increase Leafy Greens:

- Leafy greens, like spinach, kale, and Swiss chard, are highly alkaline and nutrient-dense. Incorporate them into salads, smoothies, and as side dishes.

6. Hydrate with Alkaline Beverages:

- Drink plenty of water and consider incorporating alkaline beverages like herbal teas and lemon water (lemons are acidic but have an alkalizing effect in the body).

7. Reduce Acidic Foods:

- Decrease your intake of acidic foods, such as processed foods, sugary snacks, red meat, and dairy products. While you don't have to eliminate them entirely, reducing their consumption can help achieve a better acid-alkaline balance.

8. Whole Grains:

- Choose whole grains like quinoa, millet, and amaranth, which are more alkaline-forming compared to refined grains.

9. Plant-Based Proteins:

- Opt for plant-based protein sources like legumes (e.g., lentils, chickpeas), tofu, and tempeh. These protein sources are generally more alkaline.

10. Alkaline Snacks:

- Have alkaline snacks readily available, such as raw nuts and seeds, fresh fruit, and vegetable sticks with hummus.

11. Meal Planning:

- Plan your meals in advance to ensure you have access to alkaline foods. A well-thought-out meal plan can help you make healthier choices.

12. Experiment with Alkaline Recipes:

- Explore alkaline-friendly recipes that incorporate a variety of alkaline ingredients. This can make your transition more enjoyable and sustainable.

13. Monitor Your Progress:

- Keep a record of your dietary changes and monitor how they make you feel. Be mindful of any improvements in your energy levels, digestion, and overall well-being.

14. Seek Support:

- Consider seeking guidance from a registered dietitian or nutritionist, especially if you have specific dietary needs or health goals. They can provide personalized advice to ensure you are meeting your nutritional requirements.

15. Be Patient:

- Transitioning to a new way of eating takes time. Be patient with yourself and allow room for occasional indulgences or foods you enjoy that may be less alkaline.

Remember that the alkaline diet is not a one-size-fits-all approach, and it may not be suitable for everyone. It's essential to maintain a balanced diet that meets your individual nutritional needs and health goals. If you have underlying health conditions or concerns, consult with a healthcare professional or registered dietitian for personalized guidance.

- **Alkaline Pantry Staples**

Building an alkaline pantry with essential staples is key to maintaining a diet focused on alkaline-forming foods. Here are some staple items to consider stocking in your alkaline pantry:

1. Alkaline Vegetables:

- Leafy Greens: Spinach, kale, Swiss chard, and arugula are excellent choices.

- Root Vegetables: Include sweet potatoes and beets.

2. Alkaline Fruits:

- Citrus Fruits: Lemons and limes, despite their acidic nature, have an alkalizing effect in the body.

- Berries: Blueberries, strawberries, and raspberries are alkaline options.

3. Alkaline Whole Grains:

- Quinoa: A complete protein and alkaline grain.

- Millet: A nutritious and alkaline whole grain.

- Amaranth: High in protein and alkaline-forming.

4. Alkaline Nuts and Seeds:

- Almonds: A versatile and nutritious nut.

- Chia Seeds: Rich in omega-three fatty acids and fiber.

- Flaxseeds: A great source of fiber and healthy fats.

- Pumpkin Seeds: Alkaline and packed with nutrients.

5. Alkaline Legumes:

- Lentils: High in protein and fiber.

- Chickpeas: Versatile and rich in plant-based protein.

- Green Peas: A good source of vitamins and minerals.

6. Alkaline Seasonings and Herbs:

- Fresh Herbs: Basil, parsley, cilantro, and dill can add flavor and nutrition.

- Spices: Use turmeric, cumin, and coriander for seasoning dishes.

7. Alkaline Cooking Oils:

- Extra Virgin Olive Oil: A heart-healthy, alkaline option.

- Coconut Oil: Use it for cooking and baking.

8. Alkaline Beverages:

- Herbal Teas: Chamomile, peppermint, and hibiscus are good choices.

- Lemon Water: Squeeze fresh lemon into water for an alkalizing drink.

9. Alkaline Sweeteners:

- Stevia: A natural, calorie-free sweetener.

10. Alkaline Condiments:

- Apple Cider Vinegar: Choose unfiltered, raw apple cider vinegar.

11. Alkaline Snacks:

- Rice Cakes: Choose whole-grain rice cakes.

- Dried Fruits: Opt for unsweetened dried fruits like raisins and apricots.

12. Alkaline Dairy Alternatives:

- Almond Milk: A dairy-free milk option.

- Coconut Yogurt: A dairy-free probiotic alternative.

13. Alkaline Grains and Pasta:

- Brown Rice: A staple whole grain.

- Whole Wheat Pasta: Choose whole grain varieties.

14. Alkaline Canned Goods:

- Canned Tomatoes: For sauces and stews.

- Canned Beans: Including chickpeas, black beans, and kidney beans.

15. Alkaline Vinegars:

- Balsamic Vinegar: A flavorful and acidic condiment that can be used sparingly.

16. Alkaline Fermented Foods:

- Sauerkraut: A fermented vegetable that can support gut health.

17. Alkaline Grains and Flours:

- Buckwheat Flour: A gluten-free grain with an alkaline effect.

- Almond Flour: Ground almonds for baking.

18. Alkaline Superfoods:

- Spirulina: A nutrient-dense algae.

- Chlorella: A green superfood known for its alkalizing properties.

These pantry staples can form the basis for a variety of alkaline meals and recipes. Keep in mind that the balance between alkaline and acidic foods in your diet is key, and it's essential to maintain a well-rounded, balanced diet that meets your individual nutritional needs and health goals. Consult with a healthcare professional or registered dietitian for personalized guidance on incorporating alkaline foods into your eating pattern.

- **Kitchen Tools and Equipment**

To support your journey toward an alkaline diet and prepare nutritious meals, having the right kitchen tools and equipment is essential. Here's a list of items that can make your meal preparation more efficient and enjoyable:

1. Chef's Knife:

- A high-quality chef's knife is the workhorse of the kitchen and is essential for chopping, slicing, and dicing alkaline fruits and vegetables.

2. Cutting Board:

- Invest in a sturdy, non-porous cutting board to avoid cross-contamination and make meal prep more hygienic.

3. Vegetable Peeler:

- A good peeler makes it easy to remove the skin from alkaline vegetables and fruits.

4. Salad Spinner:

- This tool helps wash and dry leafy greens and other alkaline vegetables efficiently.

5. Food Processor:

- A food processor is handy for chopping, pureeing, and making sauces or dips with alkaline ingredients.

6. Blender:

- A high-speed blender is great for making alkaline smoothies, soups, and sauces. It can handle fibrous greens and nuts.

7. Juicer:

- If you enjoy fresh alkaline fruit and vegetable juices, a juicer can help extract their nutrients efficiently.

8. Grater/Zester:

- Use a grater or zester to add flavor to your dishes with citrus zest or grate alkaline ingredients like ginger or garlic.

9. Colander/Strainer:

- A colander or strainer is essential for rinsing and draining alkaline grains, legumes, and pasta.

10. Measuring Cupful and Spoons:

- Precise measurements are crucial for following alkaline recipes and maintaining dietary balance.

11. Mixing Bowls:

- A set of mixing bowls in various sizes is necessary for combining and tossing alkaline ingredients.

12. Baking Sheets and Pans:

- If you plan to bake alkaline dishes or make healthy snacks, having baking sheets and pans is important.

13. Saucepan and Pot Set:

- These are essential for cooking whole grains, legumes, and preparing alkaline soups and stews.

14. Sauté Pan:

- A sauté pan with a non-stick surface is handy for cooking alkaline vegetables and tofu.

15. Steamer Basket:

- A steamer basket allows you to steam alkaline vegetables while preserving their nutrients.

16. Thermometer:

- A kitchen thermometer can help ensure that you cook alkaline proteins, such as tofu or tempeh, to the right temperature.

17. Salad Spinner:

- A salad spinner helps wash and dry leafy greens and other alkaline vegetables efficiently.

18. Citrus Squeezer:

- For squeezing fresh lemon or lime juice, a citrus squeezer can be a useful tool.

19. Kitchen Scale:

- If you need precise measurements for your alkaline recipes, a kitchen scale can be handy.

20. Spice Grinder:

- A spice grinder is useful for grinding whole alkaline spices and seeds to enhance flavor.

21. Nut Milk Bag:

- If you make your own almond or cashew milk, a nut milk bag is useful for straining.

22. Glass Food Storage Containers:

- To store alkaline meals and ingredients, opt for glass containers that are safe for reheating and freezing.

23. Water Filter Pitcher:

- A water filter pitcher can help ensure that you have access to clean, alkaline water for cooking and drinking.

24. Non-Stick Cookware:

- Non-stick cookware makes it easier to cook with less oil, which aligns with the alkaline diet's principles.

Having these kitchen tools and equipment on hand can make it more convenient to prepare alkaline meals and incorporate nutrient-rich, whole foods into your diet. It's essential to maintain a balanced approach to nutrition, so these tools can assist you in achieving your dietary goals while enjoying the process of cooking and eating healthily.

- **Planning Alkaline Meals**

Planning alkaline meals is a thoughtful process that involves selecting foods that promote an alkaline environment in the body. Here's a guide to help you plan balanced and nutritious alkaline meals:

1. Start with Alkaline Foods:

- Prioritize alkaline-forming foods, such as leafy greens, vegetables, fruits, and some whole grains. These foods should make up the foundation of your meals.

2. Include a Variety of Vegetables:

- Load your plate with a colorful assortment of alkaline vegetables. Think spinach, kale, broccoli, carrots, bell peppers, and beets. Variety ensures a broad range of nutrients.

3. Choose Alkaline Proteins:

- Opt for plant-based proteins like legumes (lentils, chickpeas), tofu, tempeh, and quinoa. These sources are typically alkaline-forming.

4. Whole Grains and Pseudograins:

- Incorporate alkaline whole grains such as quinoa, millet, and amaranth. These grains are excellent sources of fiber and nutrients.

5. Alkaline Fruits:

- Include alkaline fruits like berries, citrus fruits, and watermelon as a refreshing addition to your meals or snacks.

6. Healthy Fats:

- Use small amounts of healthy fats, such as extra virgin olive oil and avocado, in your meals for flavor and essential nutrients.

7. Alkaline Beverages:

- Stay hydrated with alkaline beverages like herbal teas, water with lemon, and fresh vegetable juices.

8. Create Balanced Plates:

- Aim to create balanced meals with a source of protein, a variety of vegetables, and a serving of whole grains or pseudograins.

9. Go Raw:

- Incorporate raw alkaline foods like salads, smoothies, and crudité for added enzymes and vitality.

10. Avoid or Limit Acidic Foods:

- While focusing on alkaline foods, be mindful of acidic foods like red meat, dairy, and processed snacks. These can offset your efforts to maintain an alkaline balance.

11. Experiment with Alkaline Recipes:

- Explore and try new alkaline recipes that incorporate different ingredients and preparation methods to keep your meals exciting and diverse.

12. Plan Your Meals:

- Plan your meals in advance to ensure that you have access to alkaline ingredients and can make healthy choices throughout the day.

13. Mindful Eating:

- Practice mindful eating to savor your meals, eat slowly, and recognize your hunger and fullness cues.

14. Portion Control:

- Pay attention to portion sizes to avoid overeating. While alkaline foods are healthy, balance is essential.

15. Snack Wisely:

- Keep alkaline snacks on hand for when you need a quick and nutritious bite. Examples include raw nuts, fresh fruit, and vegetable sticks with hummus.

16. Listen to Your Body:

- Pay attention to how different foods make you feel. Everyone's dietary needs are unique, so adjust your alkaline meal plan to suit your individual preferences and tolerance.

17. Consult with a Registered Dietitian:

- If you have specific dietary goals, health concerns, or unique dietary requirements, consult with a registered dietitian or nutrition expert who can provide personalized guidance and support.

Remember that an alkaline diet should be a part of a balanced and varied approach to nutrition. Incorporating alkaline foods into your meals can help promote overall health and well-being. It's important to be mindful of your dietary choices and to adapt your meal planning to meet your individual needs and goals.

CHAPTER 4

ALKALINE NUTRITION FOR OPTIMAL HEALTH

- **Weight Management with Alkaline Eating**

Alkaline eating can be a part of a balanced approach to weight management, but it's important to understand that it's not a quick fix for weight loss. Instead, it promotes a healthy lifestyle and can contribute to weight management in the following ways:

1. Promotes Nutrient-Dense Foods:

- Alkaline eating encourages the consumption of nutrient-dense foods like fruits, vegetables, and whole grains. These foods are lower in calories but rich in essential nutrients, helping you feel satisfied while providing your body with vital vitamins and minerals.

2. Reduces Caloric Density:

- Many alkaline foods are naturally low in calories and high in fiber. Fiber contributes to a feeling of fullness and helps control overall calorie intake, which can be beneficial for weight management.

3. Enhances Hydration:

- Alkaline eating includes drinking plenty of water and consuming alkaline beverages like herbal teas. Staying hydrated can help control appetite and prevent confusion between thirst and hunger.

4. Encourages Whole Foods:

- The alkaline diet discourages highly processed, sugary, and fatty foods that often contribute to weight gain. By focusing on whole, unprocessed foods, you can reduce empty calorie intake.

5. Supports Satiety:

- Alkaline foods like vegetables, whole grains, and legumes are known for promoting feelings of fullness, which can prevent overeating.

6. Reduces Acidic and Inflammatory Foods:

- Alkaline eating discourages acidic and inflammatory foods like red meat, dairy, and processed snacks. These items can be linked to weight gain and chronic inflammation.

7. Promotes Balanced Meals:

- Following the alkaline diet can lead to more balanced meals with a mix of vegetables, lean proteins, and whole grains. This can help you avoid overeating any one food group.

8. Encourages Mindful Eating:

- Alkaline eating emphasizes the importance of mindfulness. Paying attention to what you eat, savoring your food, and eating slowly can help you tune into your body's hunger and fullness cues.

9. May Support Healthy Metabolism:

- Although more research is needed, some studies suggest that diets rich in alkaline foods may positively impact metabolism and energy expenditure.

10. Consistent Energy Levels:

- Alkaline eating can help stabilize blood sugar levels, reducing the likelihood of energy crashes and overeating due to sudden hunger.

11. Long-Term Lifestyle Approach:

- Alkaline eating is not a short-term diet but a long-term lifestyle approach. It encourages sustainable changes in dietary habits, which are more effective for maintaining weight over time.

- **Alkaline Nutrition for Improved Digestion**

Alkaline nutrition can potentially support improved digestion by emphasizing foods that are gentle on the digestive system and promoting a balanced pH environment in the body. Here are ways in which an alkaline diet may benefit digestion:

1. Reduces Acid Reflux:

- Alkaline foods, especially plant-based ones, can help alleviate symptoms of acid reflux and heartburn. These foods are less likely to trigger acid production in the stomach, providing relief for individuals with gastrointestinal discomfort.

2. Supports a Balanced pH Level:

- An alkaline diet aims to maintain a balanced pH level in the body. This equilibrium is essential for optimal digestive function and the body's ability to absorb nutrients efficiently.

3. Rich in Fiber content:

- Alkaline foods such as fruits and vegetables are typically high in fiber. Dietary fiber promotes regular bowel movements, prevents constipation, and supports a healthy gut.

4. Provides Digestive Enzymes:

- Raw and minimally processed alkaline foods contain digestive enzymes that can aid in breaking down food in the stomach and small intestine, improving the overall digestion process.

5. Promotes Beneficial Gut Bacteria:

- Alkaline foods are often prebiotic, meaning they support the growth of beneficial gut bacteria. A balanced gut microbiome is crucial for digestion and overall health.

6. Reduces Inflammatory Foods:

- The alkaline diet discourages highly processed and inflammatory foods. By reducing these, you may experience relief from gastrointestinal discomfort and bloating.

7. Hydration for Digestive Health:

- Drinking alkaline beverages like herbal teas and water with lemon can help maintain proper hydration, which is essential for digestive health.

8. Encourages Mindful Eating:

- Alkaline eating emphasizes mindful eating practices, such as chewing food thoroughly and savoring each bite. This can enhance digestion by allowing the body to process food more efficiently.

9. Alleviates Gastric Ulcers:

- Some studies suggest that alkaline foods may have a soothing effect on the stomach lining, potentially reducing the symptoms of gastric ulcers.

10. Reduced Risk of Gastrointestinal Disorders:

- Alkaline foods may help reduce the risk of certain gastrointestinal disorders, such as irritable bowel syndrome (IBS) or inflammatory bowel disease (IBD).

It's important to note that while an alkaline diet may offer digestive benefits, individual responses can vary. The effectiveness of this dietary approach may depend on factors like one's overall health, specific digestive conditions, and dietary preferences.

Before making significant dietary changes, especially for digestive concerns, it's advisable to consult with a healthcare professional or registered dietitian. They can provide personalized guidance and recommendations tailored to your individual digestive needs and concerns. Additionally, they can help ensure that you maintain a well-balanced and nutrient-rich diet.

- **Alkaline Nutrition and Skin Health**

Alkaline nutrition can have a positive impact on skin health by promoting a diet rich in fruits, vegetables, and other nutrient-dense foods. Here are ways in which an alkaline diet may benefit your skin:

1. Hydration:

- Alkaline nutrition emphasizes drinking plenty of water and alkaline beverages. Proper hydration is essential for maintaining skin elasticity, preventing dryness, and supporting overall skin health.

2. Anti-Inflammatory Properties:

- Alkaline foods, especially fruits and vegetables, are known for their anti-inflammatory properties. Reducing inflammation can help alleviate skin conditions such as acne, eczema, and psoriasis.

3. Rich in Antioxidants:

- Alkaline foods are typically high in antioxidants, which can protect the skin from damage caused by free radicals. This protection can help slow down the aging process and promote a healthy, youthful complexion.

4. Promotes Collagen Production:

- Some alkaline foods, like vitamin C-rich fruits and vegetables, can help stimulate collagen production in the skin. Collagen is essential for skin elasticity and firmness.

5. Supports a Balanced pH Level:

- Alkaline nutrition aims to maintain a balanced pH level in the body. A proper pH balance can help reduce the risk of skin problems like acne and other skin irritations.

6. Detoxification:

- The alkaline diet promotes detoxification through the consumption of foods that support the liver and kidney's natural cleansing functions. Detoxifying the body can help improve the appearance of the skin.

7. Healthy Fats:

- Alkaline diets typically include healthy fats such as avocados and extra virgin olive oil. These fats contribute to skin hydration and maintain the skin's natural lipid barrier.

8. Collagen-Boosting Nutrients:

- Alkaline foods like almonds, walnuts, and chia seeds provide nutrients that support collagen production and healthy skin.

9. Reduced Processed Foods:

- The alkaline diet discourages processed, sugary, and greasy foods, which can lead to skin issues like acne and premature aging.

10. Supports Gut Health:

- A balanced gut microbiome, promoted by the prebiotic nature of many alkaline foods, can help improve skin health. An imbalance in gut bacteria is associated with skin problems.

11. Antimicrobial Effects:

- Some alkaline foods, particularly garlic and onions, have natural antimicrobial properties. These can help reduce the growth of harmful skin bacteria.

12. Reduction of Allergenic Foods:

- By eliminating common allergenic foods often associated with skin problems (e.g., dairy), the alkaline diet may provide relief from conditions like acne and eczema for some individuals.

While the alkaline diet may offer skin benefits, it's essential to understand that individual responses can vary. The effectiveness of this dietary approach may depend on factors such as one's overall health, specific skin conditions, and dietary preferences.

- **Boosting Immunity with an Alkaline Diet**

An alkaline diet may contribute to a strengthened immune system by promoting the consumption of nutrient-dense foods that support overall health and well-being. Here are ways in which an alkaline diet can help boost immunity:

1. Rich in Antioxidants:

- Alkaline foods, particularly fruits and vegetables, are high in antioxidants. These compounds help neutralize harmful free radicals, reducing oxidative stress and inflammation, which can weaken the immune system.

2. Nutrient-Dense Foods:

- The alkaline diet emphasizes the consumption of nutrient-dense foods. These foods provide essential vitamins and minerals that play a key role in immune function, including vitamins A, C, D, and E, as well as zinc and selenium.

3. Supports a Balanced pH Level:

- Maintaining a balanced pH level in the body is essential for immune health. An alkaline diet aims to reduce excess acidity, which can have a negative impact on the immune system.

4. Reduces Inflammatory Foods:

- The alkaline diet discourages highly processed and inflammatory foods that can contribute to chronic inflammation. Reducing inflammation helps the immune system function optimally.

5. Promotes Healthy Gut:

- The alkaline diet includes prebiotic foods that support a healthy gut microbiome. A balanced gut microbiome is closely linked to immune health.

6. Supports Detoxification:

- Alkaline foods promote the natural detoxification processes of the liver and kidneys. A well-functioning detoxification system is essential for removing toxins and supporting the immune system.

7. Hydration:

- Staying properly hydrated is crucial for immune health. Alkaline nutrition encourages drinking plenty of water and alkaline beverages to maintain hydration.

8. Healthy Fats:

- Alkaline diets include healthy fats like avocados and extra virgin olive oil. These fats are essential for immune function and overall health.

9. Reduces Processed Glucose content:

- Highly processed sugars can impair immune function. An alkaline diet encourages a reduction in sugar consumption, supporting a strong immune system.

10. Whole Foods:

- Whole, unprocessed foods contain a wide range of phytonutrients that contribute to immune health. These foods are central to an alkaline diet.

11. Reduces Allergenic Foods:

- The alkaline diet may help individuals with food sensitivities or allergies. By avoiding allergenic foods, it can reduce the burden on the immune system.

12. Alkaline Minerals:

- Alkaline foods are often rich in minerals like magnesium and potassium, which are essential for immune function and overall well-being.

13. Stress Reduction:

- Alkaline nutrition promotes a balanced lifestyle. Reducing stress and promoting mental well-being can have a positive impact on the immune system.

While the alkaline diet can contribute to immune support, it's important to remember that no single dietary approach is a magic bullet for immunity. A holistic approach to health, which includes a balanced diet, regular physical activity, stress management, and adequate sleep, is essential for maintaining a robust immune system.

If you have specific immune concerns or health conditions, consult with a healthcare professional or registered dietitian who can provide personalized guidance and ensure that your nutritional needs are met while helping you strengthen your immune system.

- **Alkaline Eating for Increased Energy and Vitality**

Alkaline eating can potentially enhance your energy levels and overall vitality by promoting a diet rich in nutrient-dense foods that support physical and mental well-being. Here's how an alkaline diet may boost your energy and vitality:

1. Proper Hydration:

- Alkaline eating encourages adequate hydration with water and alkaline beverages. Staying well-hydrated is essential for maintaining energy levels and overall vitality.

2. Nutrient-Dense Foods:

- The alkaline diet prioritizes nutrient-dense foods, including fruits and vegetables. These foods provide essential vitamins and minerals that are crucial for energy production and overall health.

3. Reduces Inflammatory Foods:

- By minimizing inflammatory and processed foods, an alkaline diet helps reduce the burden on the body's systems, promoting overall vitality.

4. Balanced pH Level:

- Maintaining a balanced pH level in the body is important for energy production and metabolic functions. Alkaline eating aims to keep the body's pH in check, supporting vitality.

5. Antioxidants:

- Alkaline foods are typically rich in antioxidants. These compounds help protect the body from oxidative stress, which can drain energy and lead to fatigue.

6. Promotes Digestive Health:

- An alkaline diet can support digestive health by emphasizing fiber-rich foods, prebiotics, and digestive enzymes. A healthy gut contributes to energy production and vitality.

7. Reduces Acidic Load:

- The alkaline diet helps reduce excess acidity in the body, which can lead to fatigue and a lack of vitality.

8. Supports Detoxification:

- Alkaline foods promote the natural detoxification processes of the liver and kidneys. Effective detoxification can help rid the body of toxins that may sap your energy.

9. Healthy Fats:

- Alkaline diets include healthy fats like avocados and extra virgin olive oil, which provide sustained energy and support overall vitality.

10. Stress Reduction:

- Alkaline nutrition is often part of a balanced lifestyle. Stress management and a focus on mental well-being can improve energy levels and vitality.

11. Whole Foods:

- Alkaline diets emphasize whole, unprocessed foods that provide a balanced source of energy and maintain stable blood sugar levels.

CHAPTER 5

SHOPPING FOR ALKALINE FOODS

- **Understanding Food Labels**

Food labels are an essential tool for consumers to make informed choices about the products they purchase. Understanding food labels can help you assess the nutritional content of a product and make healthier choices. Some key information found on food labels includes:

- **Nutrition Facts:** This section provides information about serving size, calories, and the amounts of macronutrients (carbohydrates, fats, proteins) and micronutrients (vitamins and minerals) in the product.

- **Ingredients List:** The ingredients list lists all the components of the product in descending order by weight. It helps you identify what the product contains and whether it includes any allergens or additives.

- **Percent Daily Value (%DV):** The %DV tells you how much a nutrient in a serving of food contributes to your daily diet. It's based on a daily intake of 2,000 calories, which is the reference used on food labels in many countries.

- **Serving Size:** Pay attention to the serving size, as it can affect the accuracy of the nutrition information. If you consume more or less than the specified serving size, adjust the nutritional values accordingly.

- **Nutrient Claims:** Look for nutrient content claims such as "low-fat," "high-fiber," or "sugar-free." These claims provide information about specific nutrients in the product.

- **Allergen Warnings:** Manufacturers are required to label common allergens like peanuts, tree nuts, milk, eggs, wheat, soy, fish, and shellfish. Check this section if you have allergies.

- **Expiration Date or Best By Date:** This information is crucial for food safety. Consuming food past its expiration date can pose health risks.

- **Net Weight:** It tells you the weight of the product, which can be helpful for comparing similar products and assessing value for money.

Organic vs. Conventional Produce:

The choice between organic and conventional produce depends on various factors, including your personal preferences, budget, and environmental concerns. Here's a comparison of the two:

- **Organic Produce:** Organic fruits and vegetables are grown without synthetic pesticides, herbicides, and genetically modified organisms (GMOs). Organic farming practices also prioritize soil health and biodiversity. Organic produce can be more expensive, but some people choose it for its reduced exposure to pesticides and perceived environmental benefits.

- **Conventional Produce:** Conventional fruits and vegetables are grown using synthetic chemicals to control pests and promote growth. They are generally more affordable than organic produce. While they may have pesticide residues, government regulations ensure that these residues are within safe limits.

When choosing between organic and conventional produce, consider your budget, priorities, and the specific fruits and vegetables you're buying. You can also use resources like the Environmental Working Group's "Dirty Dozen" and "Clean Fifteen" lists to identify which produce items are more likely to have pesticide residues and may be worth buying organic.

Seasonal and Local Alkaline Foods:

Eating seasonal and locally sourced alkaline foods can have several benefits:

- **Freshness:** Seasonal foods are typically harvested at their peak ripeness, making them fresher and more flavorful.

- **Nutrient Density:** Seasonal foods often have higher nutrient content because they spend less time in transit and storage.

- **Environmental Impact:** Buying local and seasonal foods can reduce the carbon footprint associated with transporting and storing out-of-season produce.

- **Supporting Local Economy:** Purchasing locally sourced foods can support local farmers and the community.

To find seasonal and local alkaline foods, visit farmers' markets, join a Community Supported Agriculture (CSA) program, or look for local and regional produce in your grocery store. Additionally, you can research seasonal charts for your area to identify when specific alkaline foods are in season.

Budget-Friendly Alkaline Shopping

Eating an alkaline diet doesn't have to break the bank. With careful planning and smart choices, you can incorporate alkaline foods into your diet without overspending. Here are some tips for budget-friendly alkaline shopping:

1. Plan Your Meals:

- Before you shop, plan your meals for the week. This allows you to create a shopping list and avoid buying unnecessary items.

2. Buy in Bulk:

- Purchase alkaline staples like grains, legumes, nuts, and seeds in bulk. This often comes at a lower cost per unit and reduces packaging waste.

3. Seasonal and Local Produce:

- Focus on seasonal and locally sourced fruits and vegetables, as they tend to be more affordable. Farmers' markets can be a great place to find fresh, local produce.

4. Frozen and Canned Produce:

- Don't hesitate to buy frozen or canned fruits and vegetables when fresh options are expensive or not in season. They are often more budget-friendly and have a longer shelf life.

5. Store Brands:

- Consider purchasing store brand or generic products rather than name brands, as they are usually more cost-effective.

6. Compare Prices:

- Compare prices at different stores and look for sales and discounts. Shopping at discount or bulk stores can often save you money.

7. Minimize Waste:

- Be mindful of food waste. Use leftovers, plan meals to use perishable items first, and freeze excess portions for future use.

8. DIY Snacks:

- Make your own alkaline snacks like almond butter, kale chips, and energy bars. This can be more cost-effective than buying pre-packaged snacks.

9. Cook at Home:

- Cooking meals at home is generally more economical than eating out. Experiment with alkaline recipes and meal prep to save time and money.

10. Grow Your Own:

- If possible, consider growing your own alkaline herbs, fruits, and vegetables. Home gardening can be a budget-friendly way to access fresh produce.

11. Prioritize High-Alkaline Foods:

- Focus on high-alkaline foods like leafy greens, cruciferous vegetables, and alkaline grains to maximize the benefits of your diet.

12. Store Properly:

- Learn how to store alkaline foods to extend their shelf life and prevent waste. Proper storage can save you money in the long run.

Alkaline Food Storage and Preservation:

Properly storing and preserving alkaline foods is essential to minimize waste and maintain their nutritional value. Here are some guidelines for storing and preserving alkaline foods:

1. Refrigeration:

- Store most alkaline vegetables, such as leafy greens, broccoli, and bell peppers, in the refrigerator's crisper drawer to maintain freshness.

2. Dry Storage:

- Alkaline grains like quinoa and millet, as well as nuts and seeds, can be stored in a cool, dry place in airtight containers. Keep them away from heat and direct sunlight.

3. Freezing:

- If you have a surplus of alkaline foods, consider freezing them. Blanch vegetables before freezing to preserve their quality.

4. Canning:

- Canning is an excellent way to preserve alkaline foods like tomatoes and some fruits. Follow proper canning procedures to ensure safety.

5. Fermentation:

- Fermenting vegetables like sauerkraut or kimchi can extend their shelf life while providing probiotic benefits.

6. Dehydrating:

- Dehydrating fruits and vegetables can result in long-lasting snacks that retain their alkaline properties.

7. Use Glass Containers:

- Store alkaline foods in glass containers rather than plastic to prevent chemical leaching and maintain purity.

8. Label and Date:

- Label stored items with the date of storage to help keep track of freshness.

9. Keep Citrus Separate:

- Citrus fruits release ethylene gas, which can lead to spoilage in other fruits and vegetables. Store them separately.

10. Follow Recommendations:

- Follow specific storage recommendations for each type of alkaline food to ensure it stays fresh.

Chapter 6

Alkaline Breakfast Delights

1. Alkaline Green Smoothie

Ingredients:

- two cupful of spinach

- one cucumber, peeled and sliced

- one green apple, cored and sliced

- half lemon, juiced

- one cupful of water

- one tablespoonful of chia seeds

- Ice cubes

Instructions:

1. Combine water, lemon juice, spinach, cucumber, green apple, and spinach into a blender.

2. Whisk together to the point of smoothness. To make the smoothie cooler, ice cubes may be added.

3. To thicken, let the glass aside for a few minutes after pouring and then whisk in some chia seeds.

4. Here's to your revitalizing green alkaline smoothie!

Duration: five minutes

Nutrients: Caloric content: 150 Amino content: 4g Carb content: 30g Fiber content: 9g Glucose content: 16g Fatty acid: 3g

2. Quinoa Breakfast Bowl

Ingredients:

- one cupful quinoa

- two cupful almond milk (or any alkaline-friendly milk)

- one banana, sliced

- one-fourth cupful fresh blueberries

- one-fourth cupful chopped almonds

- one tablespoonful honey

- half teaspoonful cinnamon

Instructions:

1. Cook the quinoa in the almond milk as directed on the box.
2. Once the quinoa is done cooking, place it in a bowl.
3. Layer in blueberries, almonds, and banana slices.
4. Honey and cinnamon may be added at this point, if you want.
5. Breakfast quinoa bowls should be served hot.

Duration: twenty minutes

Nutrients: Caloric content: 400 Amino content: 11g Carb content: 65g Fiber content: 9g Glucose content: 17g Fatty acid: 14g

3. Chia Pudding with Berries

Ingredients:

- two tablespoonful chia seeds

- one cupful almond milk (or any alkaline-friendly milk)

- half teaspoonful vanilla extract

- half cupful mixed berries (e.g., strawberries, blueberries, raspberries)

Instructions:

1. Mix almond milk, vanilla essence, and chia seeds in a bowl.
2. Mix well, cover, and chill for at least three hours, preferably overnight, until thick.
3. Serve chia pudding with fresh berries for breakfast.
4. Have a breakfast that will fuel you for the day.

Duration: Overnight or three hours

Nutrients: Caloric content: two hundred and twenty Amino content: 5g Carb content: 25g Fiber content: 12g Glucose content: 7g Fatty acid: 11g

4. Alkaline Oatmeal

Ingredients:

- one cupful steel-cut oats

- two cupful water

- half cupful almond milk (or any alkaline-friendly milk)

- one-fourth teaspoonful cinnamon

- half cupful sliced bananas

- one-fourth cupful chopped walnuts

- one tablespoonful maple syrup

Instructions:

1. Put some water on to boil in a pot.
2. When the water has returned to a simmer, add the steel-cut oats.
3. Stirring periodically, oats need to cook for approximately half an hour.

4. Banana slices, almond milk, and cinnamon should be mixed together.

5. Sprinkle some chopped walnuts and maple syrup on top.

Duration: thirty minutes

Nutrients: Caloric content: 380 Amino content: 9g Carb content: 54g Fiber content: 9g Glucose content: 13g Fatty acid: 15g

5. Avocado and Tomato Toast

Ingredients:

- two slices of whole-grain or alkaline-friendly bread

- one ripe avocado

- one tomato, sliced

- one-fourth red onion, thinly sliced

- one tablespoonful fresh lemon juice

- Salt and pepper to taste

- Fresh basil leaves for garnish

Instructions:

1. Toasted bread should have a golden brown color.

2. The ripe avocado should be mashed in a bowl with the addition of lemon juice, salt, and pepper.

3. After toasting the bread, spread the avocado mixture on it.

4. Sliced tomatoes, red onion, and basil leaves make a great topping.

5. To make a filling breakfast, serve your avocado and tomato toast.

Duration: ten minutes

Nutrients: Caloric content: 280 Amino content: 6g Carb content: 30g Fiber content: 10g Glucose content: 3g Fatty acid: 17g

6. Alkaline Veggie Omelette

Ingredients:

- three large eggs

- half cupful diced bell peppers

- half cupful diced tomatoes

- one-fourth cupful diced red onion

- one-fourth cupful spinach leaves

- Salt and pepper to taste

- one tablespoonful olive oil

Instructions:

1. The eggs should be beaten in a bowl and then seasoned with salt and pepper.
2. Olive oil should be heated in a nonstick pan over medium heat.
3. Sprinkle in some spinach, red onion, tomatoes, and bell peppers. Stir-fry for a minute or two.
4. The eggs should be poured over the vegetables and cooked until they set.
5. The omelet should be served folded in half and heated.

Duration: ten minutes

Nutrients: Caloric content: 290 Amino content: 14g Carb content: 11g Fiber content: 3g Glucose content: 5g Fatty acid: 21g

7. Alkaline Pancakes

Ingredients:

- one cupful spelt flour

- one teaspoonful baking powder

- one ripe banana, mashed

- one cupful almond milk (or any alkaline-friendly milk)

- one tablespoonful coconut oil

- one teaspoonful vanilla extract

- Fresh berries for topping

Instructions:

1. Combine the spelt flour and baking soda in a bowl and mix well.

2. Put the mashed bananas, almond milk, coconut oil, and vanilla extract in a separate dish and mix well.

3. Blend the batter by combining the wet and dry components.

4. Pancakes may be made by heating a nonstick skillet over medium heat and then spooning in the batter.

5. Bubbles should appear on the surface before you turn it over to cook the other side.

6. Put some ripe berries over top and serve.

Duration: fifteen minutes

Nutrients: Caloric content: 3twenty Amino content: 7g Carb content: 50g Fiber content: 7g Glucose content: 9g Fatty acid: 11g

8. Alkaline Acai Bowl

Ingredients:

- two frozen acai smoothie packs

- half cupful almond milk (or any alkaline-friendly milk)

- one ripe banana

- half cupful mixed berries

- two tablespoonful granola

- one tablespoonful chia seeds

Instructions:

1. Frozen acai packets, almond milk, a banana, and half the mixed berries should be blended together.

2. Whisk together to the point of smoothness.

3. The acai smoothie should be served in a bowl.

4. Mix the remaining berries, granola, and chia seeds and sprinkle over top.

5. Sup on that healthy acai bowl.

Duration: five minutes

Nutrients: Caloric content: 3twenty Amino content: 6g Carb content: 46g Fiber content: 10g Glucose content: 20g Fatty acid: 14g

9. Alkaline Chia Seed Smoothie

Ingredients:

- one tablespoonful chia seeds

- one cupful almond milk (or any alkaline-friendly milk)

- half cupful fresh pineapple chunks

- half cupful kale leaves

- half teaspoonful ginger, grated

- half teaspoonful turmeric

- Honey or maple syrup for sweetness

Instructions:

1. Let the chia seeds and almond milk soak together for 10 minutes in a glass.
2. Add the chia mixture, pineapple, kale, ginger, and turmeric to a blender and process until smooth.
3. Whisk together to the point of smoothness. To taste, sweeten with honey or maple syrup.
4. Smoothie made with chia seeds; pour into a glass and savor.

Duration: ten minutes (including chia seed soaking) **Nutrients:** Caloric content: 180 Amino content: 4g Carb content: 32g Fiber content: 10g Glucose content: 13g Fatty acid: 6g

10. Alkaline Avocado Toast with Hemp Seeds

Ingredients:

- two slices of whole-grain or alkaline-friendly bread

- one ripe avocado

- two tablespoonful hemp seeds

- A pinch of red pepper flakes

- Salt and pepper to taste

Instructions:

1. Toasted bread should have a golden brown color.

2. Spread the ripe avocado on bread by mashing it.

3. Hemp seeds, crushed red pepper, salt, and pepper.

4. Toast avocados for a fast and nutritious morning meal.

Duration: ten minutes

Nutrients: Caloric content: 3thirty Amino content: 10g Carb content: 21g Fiber content: 9g Glucose content: 1g Fatty acid: 25g

11. Alkaline Overnight Oats

Ingredients:

- half cupful rolled oats

- one cupful almond milk (or any alkaline-friendly milk)

- half teaspoonful vanilla extract

- half cupful sliced strawberries

- one-fourth cupful sliced almonds

- one tablespoonful maple syrup

Instructions:

1. Put the rolled oats, almond milk, and vanilla essence into a container and shake well.

2. Mix with some strawberry slices and almond slices.

3. Refrigerate the jar, sealed, for at least 12 hours.

4. You may top your overnight oats with maple syrup in the morning if you choose.

Duration: Overnight **Nutrients:** Caloric content: 300 Amino content: 8g Carb content: 35g Fiber content: 7g Glucose content: 8g Fatty acid: 15g

12. Alkaline Berry Parfait

Ingredients:

- half cupful mixed berries (e.g., blueberries, strawberries, raspberries)

- half cupful almond yogurt (or any alkaline-friendly yogurt)

- one-fourth cupful granola

- one tablespoonful flax seeds

- one teaspoonful honey

Instructions:

1. Layer almond yoghurt and mixed berries in a glass or dish.
2. Granola and flax seeds make a great topping.
3. Honey may be used as a finishing touch.
4. Put out the door with your berry parfait.

Duration: five minutes

Nutrients: Caloric content: 3twenty Amino content: 7g Carb content: 45g Fiber content: 9g Glucose content: 18g Fatty acid: 13g

13. Alkaline Breakfast Burrito

Ingredients:

- two large collard green leaves

- four scrambled eggs

- half cupful black beans, cooked and drained

- one-fourth cupful diced tomatoes

- one-fourth cupful diced red onion

- one-fourth cupful sliced avocado

- Salsa for serving

Instructions:

1. To soften the collard green leaves, steam them for 1–2 minutes.
2. Arrange the scrambled eggs, black beans, tomatoes, red onion, and avocado on a flat bed of collard green leaves.
3. Make burritos out of the leaves by rolling them up.
4. To enhance the flavor, drizzle with salsa.

Duration: ten minutes

Nutrients: Caloric content: 3thirty Amino content: 17g Carb content: 32g Fiber content: 10g Glucose content: 3g Fatty acid: 16g

14. Alkaline Banana Walnut Muffins

Ingredients:

- one half cupful spelt flour

- half cupful almond milk (or any alkaline-friendly milk)

- two ripe bananas, mashed

- one-fourth cupful chopped walnuts

- one-fourth cupful maple syrup

- one-fourth cupful coconut oil

- one teaspoonful baking powder

Instructions:

1. Have a muffin tray ready and heat the oven to 350 degrees Fahrenheit (175 degrees Celsius).
2. Mix baking powder with spelt flour in a bowl.
3. Bananas should be mashed and then combined with almond milk, maple syrup, and melted coconut oil in a separate dish.
4. Combine the wet and dry ingredients by stirring until just incorporated, then folding in the chopped walnuts.
5. Distribute the mixture evenly among the muffin cups.
6. Bake until a toothpick inserted in the center comes out clean, about 25 minutes.
7. Please wait till the muffins have cooled before eating.

Duration: Twenty Five minutes

Nutrients: Caloric content: 180 Amino content: 3g Carb content: 22g Fiber content: 3g Glucose content: 9g Fatty acid: 9g

15. Alkaline Breakfast Tofu Scramble

Ingredients:

- half block of firm tofu, crumbled

- half cupful chopped bell peppers

- half cupful chopped zucchini

- one-fourth cupful chopped red onion

- one-fourth cupful spinach leaves

- one-fourth teaspoonful turmeric

- Salt and pepper to taste

- one tablespoonful olive oil

Instructions:

1. Olive oil should be heated in a pan over medium heat.
2. Toss in some zucchini, red onion and red pepper chunks. Stir-fry for a minute or two.
3. Then, stir in the tofu, turmeric, salt, and pepper. Heat the tofu for a suitable amount of time.
4. Cook the spinach leaves by stirring them in until they wilt.
5. Keep the heat on for your tofu scramble.

Duration: fifteen minutes

Nutrients: Caloric content: 280 Amino content: 12g Carb content: 14g Fiber content: 5g Glucose content: 4g Fatty acid: 20g

16. Alkaline Buckwheat Pancakes

Ingredients:

- one cupful buckwheat flour

- one teaspoonful baking powder

- half cupful almond milk (or any alkaline-friendly milk)

- one ripe banana, mashed

- one teaspoonful vanilla extract

- Fresh berries for topping

- one tablespoonful coconut oil

Instructions:

1. Buckwheat flour and baking powder should be mixed together in a bowl.

2. Put the mashed banana, almond milk, and vanilla essence in a separate dish and mix well.

3. Blend the batter by combining the wet and dry components.

4. Coconut oil should be heated in a nonstick pan over medium heat.

5. Cook the pancakes until bubbles appear on the surface, then flip. To finish cooking, turn the food over.

6. Put some ripe berries over top and serve.

Duration: fifteen minutes

Nutrients: Caloric content: 3thirty Amino content: 8g Carb content: 54g Fiber content: 8g Glucose content: 11g Fatty acid: 10g

17. Alkaline Berry Smoothie Bowl

Ingredients:

- one cupful mixed berries (e.g., blueberries, strawberries, raspberries)

- half ripe banana

- half cupful almond milk (or any alkaline-friendly milk)

- one tablespoonful chia seeds

- one tablespoonful almond butter

- one-fourth cupful granola

Instructions:

1. Blend together chia seeds, almond butter, almond milk, frozen banana, and mixed berries.

2. Whisk together to the point of smoothness.

3. The smoothie should be served in a bowl.

4. Granola is a great topping since it adds crunch and nutrients.

5. Take pleasure in your healthy smoothie bowl.

Duration: five minutes

Nutrients: Caloric content: 380 Amino content: 8g Carb content: 56g Fiber content: 13g Glucose content: 19g

CHAPTER 7

LUNCH AND DINNER CREATIONS

18. Alkaline Quinoa Salad

Ingredients:

- one cupful quinoa

- two cupful water

- one cucumber, diced

- one red bell pepper, diced

- one cupful cherry tomatoes, halved

- one-fourth red onion, thinly sliced

- one-fourth cupful fresh parsley, chopped

- Juice of one lemon

- two tablespoonful extra-virgin olive oil

- Salt and pepper to taste

Instructions:

1. In a fine-mesh sieve, thoroughly rinse the quinoa.
2. Put the quinoa and water in a medium pot and let it simmer. Cook for 15–20 minutes at a low simmer until the quinoa is tender and the water is absorbed after being brought to a boil.
3. After cooking quinoa, fluff it with a fork and set it aside to cool.
4. Quinoa, cucumber, red bell pepper, cherry tomatoes, red onion, and fresh parsley should be mixed together in a big bowl.
5. Lemon juice and olive oil should be mixed separately. Use salt and pepper to taste.
6. Toss the salad with the dressing to coat.
7. Your alkaline quinoa salad is a great main course or side dish.

Duration: Twenty Five-thirty minutes

Nutrients: Caloric content: 3thirty Amino content: 8g Carb content: 51g Fiber content: 6g Glucose content: 3g Fatty acid: 11g

19. Alkaline Chickpea and Spinach Curry

Ingredients:

- one can (fifteen oz) chickpeas, drained and rinsed

- one onion, chopped

- two cloves garlic, minced

- one can (1four oz) diced tomatoes

- two cupful fresh spinach

- one tablespoonful curry powder

- one teaspoonful ground cumin

- one teaspoonful ground turmeric

- half teaspoonful ground coriander

- half teaspoonful chili flakes (adjust to taste)

- one cupful alkaline-friendly vegetable broth

- one tablespoonful coconut oil

- Salt and pepper to taste

Instructions:

1. Coconut oil should be heated over medium heat in a big skillet.
2. Sauté the onion chunks until they become transparent.
3. Mix in some curry powder, cumin, turmeric, coriander, and chilli flakes, along with some chopped garlic. Add the spices and cook for 1–2 minutes.
4. Add tomato paste and broth made from vegetables. Get it to a low boil.
5. After ten to fifteen minutes, when the sauce has thickened, add the chickpeas.
6. Cook fresh spinach by folding it in and letting it wilt.
7. Use salt and pepper to taste.
8. Brown rice or quinoa might go well with your alkaline chickpea and spinach dish.

Duration: thirty minutes

Nutrients: Caloric content: 3twenty Amino content: 12g Carb content: 46g Fiber content: 11g Glucose content: 10g Fatty acid: 10g

20. Alkaline Stir-Fried Vegetables with Tofu

Ingredients:

- one block of tofu, cubed

- two cupful broccoli florets

- one red bell pepper, sliced

- one yellow bell pepper, sliced

- one small zucchini, sliced

- one small onion, sliced

- three cloves garlic, minced

- two tablespoonful tamari or coconut proteins

- one tablespoonful olive oil

- one teaspoonful ginger, minced

- Salt and pepper to taste

Instructions:

1. Olive oil should be heated over medium heat in a big skillet.
2. Stir-fry the tofu cubes until they're brown and crispy. Don't bother with right now.
3. Garlic and ginger should be minced and added to the same pan. Warm up in a skillet for a minute.
4. Throw in some chopped onion, peppers, broccoli and zucchini. Cook in a wok for 5–7 minutes, or until tender but still crisp.
5. Put the tofu back in the pan and top it with some tamari or coconut protein.
6. To heat the tofu and combine the flavours, continue cooking for another two to three minutes.
7. Use salt and pepper to taste.
8. Top quinoa or brown rice with your alkaline stir-fried veggies and tofu.

Duration: twenty minutes

Nutrients: Caloric content: 350 Amino content: 18g Carb content: 25g Fiber content: 6g Glucose content: 6g Fatty acid: 21g

21. Alkaline Lentil and Vegetable Soup

Ingredients:

- one cupful green or brown lentils, rinsed

- four cupful alkaline-friendly vegetable broth

- one onion, diced

- two carrots, diced

- two celery stalks, diced

- one zucchini, diced

- one can (1four oz) diced tomatoes

- two cloves garlic, minced

- one teaspoonful cumin

- one teaspoonful paprika

- half teaspoonful turmeric

- half teaspoonful coriander

- Salt and pepper to taste

Instructions:

1. Olive oil should be heated over medium heat in a big saucepan.
2. Chop some onion, carrots, celery and zucchini, and add them to the pot. Cook for 5 to 7 minutes in a sauté pan until they start to soften.
3. Add the minced garlic and continue cooking for another minute.
4. Put in the lentils, tomato chunks, vegetable stock, and all the seasonings.
5. To cook the lentils, bring the ingredients to a boil, then decrease the heat and cover the pot for 25–30 minutes.
6. Taste and adjust salt and pepper.
7. Put some fresh lemon juice on the side of your alkaline lentil and vegetable soup.

Duration: 40 minutes

Nutrients: Caloric content: 240 Amino content: 15g Carb content: 40g Fiber content: 10g Glucose content: 6g Fatty acid: 2g

22. Alkaline Spinach and Mushroom Stuffed Peppers

Ingredients:

- four bell peppers, any color

- one cupful quinoa

- two cupful alkaline-friendly vegetable broth

- one cupful mushrooms, chopped

- two cupful fresh spinach

- half cupful diced tomatoes

- one small onion, diced

- two cloves garlic, minced

- one teaspoonful olive oil

- half teaspoonful thyme

- Salt and pepper to taste

Instructions:

1. Have a 375F (190C) oven ready.
2. Remove the stems and seeds from the bell peppers.
3. Bake the peppers by putting them on a baking dish.
4. Prepare the quinoa by washing it and then cooking it in vegetable broth as directed.
5. Olive oil should be heated over medium heat in a skillet.
6. Put in the mushrooms and onions and cook for five minutes.
7. Mix in the thyme, salt, pepper, chopped garlic, spinach, and diced tomatoes. Wilt the spinach in the cooking process.
8. Mix the cooked quinoa into the sautéed spinach and mushrooms.
9. Prepare the quinoa filling and place it into the bell peppers.
10. Cook for 25–30 minutes with the foil covering the dish.
11. Present your alkaline filled peppers with spinach and mushrooms.

Duration: 40 minutes

Nutrients: Caloric content: 280 Amino content: 8g Carb content: 54g Fiber content: 8g Glucose content: 6g Fatty acid: 4g

23. Alkaline Lentil and Sweet Potato Curry

Ingredients:

- one cupful brown or green lentils, rinsed

- two cupful alkaline-friendly vegetable broth

- one large sweet potato, peeled and diced

- one can (1four oz) diced tomatoes

- one onion, chopped

- two cloves garlic, minced

- one tablespoonful curry powder

- half teaspoonful turmeric

- half teaspoonful ground cumin

- half teaspoonful paprika

- one-fourth teaspoonful chili flakes (adjust to taste)

- one tablespoonful olive oil

- Salt and pepper to taste

- Fresh cilantro for garnish

Instructions:

1. Olive oil should be heated over medium heat in a big saucepan.
2. Sauté the onion chunks until they become transparent.
3. Cook the garlic for a minute after stirring it in.
4. Throw in some sweet potatoes, lentils, chopped tomatoes, some vegetable broth, and a whole lot of spices.
5. Bring to a boil, then decrease heat and simmer until lentils and sweet potatoes are cooked, about 25-30 minutes.
6. Use salt and pepper to taste.
7. Cilantro leaves, for garnish.
8. Eat your sweet potato and lentil curry alkaline with some brown rice or quinoa.

Duration: 40 minutes

Nutrients: Caloric content: 3twenty Amino content: 13g Carb content: 60g Fiber content: 16g Glucose content: 7g Fatty acid: 5g

24. Alkaline Veggie and Quinoa Stuffed Portobello Mushrooms

Ingredients:

- four large portobello mushrooms

- one cupful quinoa

- two cupful alkaline-friendly vegetable broth

- one red bell pepper, diced

- one zucchini, diced

- one cupful spinach, chopped

- half cupful cherry tomatoes, halved

- one-fourth cupful red onion, diced

- two cloves garlic, minced

- one tablespoonful olive oil

- one teaspoonful Italian seasoning

- Salt and pepper to taste

Instructions:

1. Have a 375F (190C) oven ready.
2. The portobello mushrooms should have their stems and gills cut off.
3. Place the mushrooms, cap side up, in a baking dish.
4. Prepare the quinoa by washing it and then cooking it in vegetable broth as directed.
5. Olive oil should be heated over medium heat in a skillet.
6. Mix in some red pepper, zucchini, cherry tomatoes and sliced onion. Stir-fry for around five minutes.
7. Add chopped spinach and minced garlic and mix well. Wilt the spinach in the cooking process.
8. Mix the quinoa with the cooked vegetables.
9. Prepare the quinoa and vegetable mixture and stuff each portobello mushroom cap.
10. Season with salt, pepper, and Italian seasoning.
11. Cook for 25–30 minutes with the foil covering the dish.
12. Portobello mushrooms filled with quinoa and alkaline vegetables.

Duration: 40 minutes

Nutrients: Caloric content: 280 Amino content: 11g Carb content: 53g Fiber content: 9g Glucose content: 5g Fatty acid: 6g

25. Alkaline Spaghetti Squash with Roasted Tomato and Garlic Sauce

Ingredients:

- one spaghetti squash, halved and seeds removed

- four tomatoes, halved

- four cloves garlic

- two tablespoonful olive oil

- one-fourth cupful fresh basil leaves

- Salt and pepper to taste

- Crushed red pepper flakes for garnish

Instructions:

1. Prepare a baking dish by preheating the oven to 400 degrees Fahrenheit (200 degrees Celsius).
2. Sprinkle salt and pepper on the spaghetti squash halves and drizzle with olive oil.
3. Prepare a baking sheet with spaghetti squash, tomatoes, and garlic.
4. If you want soft squash, roast it for 40–45 minutes.
5. Take the roasted squash out of the oven and use a fork to scrape the threads apart.
6. To make the sauce, place the roasted tomatoes, roasted garlic, fresh basil, and a dash of olive oil in a blender and mix until smooth. Whisk together to the point of smoothness.
7. Roast the tomatoes and garlic, then use that sauce to top the spaghetti squash.
8. Add some spice with crushed red pepper flakes or fresh basil leaves as garnish.

Duration: one hour **Nutrients:** Caloric content: two hundred and twenty Amino content: 4g Carb content: 38g Fiber content: 8g Glucose content: 11g Fatty acid: 8g

26. Alkaline Baked Stuffed Eggplant

Ingredients:

- two large eggplants

- one cupful quinoa

- two cupful alkaline-friendly vegetable broth

- one can (1four oz) diced tomatoes

- one onion, diced

- two cloves garlic, minced

- half cupful fresh basil leaves, chopped

- one-fourth cupful pine nuts

- one-fourth cupful nutritional yeast (optional, for a cheesy flavor)

- two tablespoonful olive oil

- Salt and pepper to taste

Instructions:

1. Have a 375F (190C) oven ready.
2. Split the eggplants in half vertically, and then use a spoon to remove the meat, leaving a shell.
3. Put the aubergine halves in a baking tray.
4. Prepare the quinoa by washing it and then cooking it in vegetable broth as directed.
5. Olive oil should be heated over medium heat in a skillet.
6. When the onion is transparent, add it to the pan.
7. Cook the garlic for a minute after stirring it in.
8. Cook the chopped aubergine flesh for 5–7 minutes, or until it reaches the desired tenderness.
9. Mix together the cooked quinoa, eggplant combination, chopped tomatoes, fresh basil, pine nuts and nutritional yeast (if using).
10. Fill the quinoa mixture into the eggplant cups.
11. After 30–35 minutes, remove the foil and uncover the dish.
12. Alkaline cooked stuffed aubergine, please.

Duration: forty five minutes

Nutrients: Caloric content: 280 Amino content: 10g Carb content: 46g Fiber content: 10g Glucose content: 8g Fatty acid: 7g

27. Alkaline Vegetable and Lentil Stir-Fry

Ingredients:

- one cupful green or brown lentils, rinsed

- two cupful alkaline-friendly vegetable broth

- one red bell pepper, sliced

- one yellow bell pepper, sliced

- one zucchini, sliced

- one cupful broccoli florets

- one cupful snap peas

- half cupful carrots, sliced

- one-fourth cupful red onion, sliced

- three cloves garlic, minced

- two tablespoonful tamari or coconut proteins

- one tablespoonful olive oil

- one teaspoonful ginger, minced

- Salt and pepper to taste

Instructions:

1. Olive oil should be heated over medium heat in a big skillet.
2. Put in some red onion slices and cook until they become transparent.
3. Mix with some ginger and chopped garlic. Stir-fry for a minute.
4. Stir-fry all the cut veggies for 7-10 minutes, or until they are soft yet still crunchy.
5. Cook the lentils in the veggie broth as directed on the box.
6. Stir the cooked lentils into the veggie stir-fry.
7. Toss the ingredients with some tamari or coconut proteins.
8. Keep it in the oven for another two or three minutes to let the flavours mingle.
9. Use salt and pepper to taste.
10. Toss in some lentils and some alkaline vegetables and serve.

Duration: thirty five minutes

Nutrients: Caloric content: 3twenty Amino content: 14g Carb content: 53g Fiber content: 15g Glucose content: 6g Fatty acid: 5g

28. Alkaline Spinach and Tomato Spaghetti

Ingredients:

- 8 oz (about two cupful) whole-grain or alkaline-friendly spaghetti

- two cupful fresh spinach

- one cupful cherry tomatoes, halved

- three cloves garlic, minced

- one-fourth cupful fresh basil leaves, chopped

- two tablespoonful olive oil

- Salt and pepper to taste

- Nutritional yeast for garnish

Instructions:

1. Prepare the spaghetti in accordance with the directions on the box.
2. Olive oil should be heated over medium heat in a big skillet.
3. Put in some minced garlic and cook it for a minute.
4. Fresh spinach and cherry tomatoes should be added. The spinach and tomatoes should be cooked until they are just tender.
5. Use salt and pepper to taste.
6. Put the veggies in a pan and add the cooked spaghetti, which has been drained.
7. Blend with some fresh basil.
8. If you like a cheese flavour, sprinkle nutritional yeast on top.
9. Put out the alkaline pasta with spinach and tomatoes.

Duration: twenty minutes

Nutrients: Caloric content: 3twenty Amino content: 9g Carb content: 50g Fiber content: 10g Glucose content: 4g Fatty acid: 9g

29. Alkaline Baked Sweet Potato Fries

Ingredients:

- two large sweet potatoes, cut into fries

- two tablespoonful olive oil

- half teaspoonful paprika

- half teaspoonful garlic powder

- half teaspoonful onion powder

- Salt and pepper to taste

Instructions:

1. Have a 425F (220C) oven ready.
2. Olive oil, paprika, garlic powder, onion powder, salt, and pepper should be combined with the sweet potato fries in a big dish.
3. Create a single layer of fries on a baking pan.
4. To get a crisp and golden brown exterior, bake for 25–30 minutes, flipping once.
5. Make a nutritious side dish or midday snack out of your alkaline fried sweet potato fries.

Duration: thirty five minutes

Nutrients: Caloric content: two hundred and twenty Amino content: 2g Carb content: 30g Fiber content: 5g Glucose content: 6g Fatty acid: 10g

30. Alkaline Cucumber and Avocado Gazpacho

Ingredients:

- two cucumbers, peeled and chopped

- two ripe avocados, peeled and pitted

- one green bell pepper, chopped

- one-fourth red onion, chopped

- two cloves garlic, minced

- two tablespoonful fresh lemon juice

- two cupful alkaline-friendly vegetable broth

- one-fourth cupful fresh cilantro leaves

- Salt and pepper to taste

Instructions:

1. Cucumbers, avocados, green pepper, red onion, minced garlic, lemon juice, and vegetable broth should all be blended together in a food processor or high-powered blender.
2. Mix it up until it's nice and creamy.
3. Taste and adjust salt and pepper.
4. Put in the fridge and let it chill for at least an hour.
5. Add some fresh cilantro to your alkaline cucumber and avocado gazpacho and serve it to your guests.

Duration: fifteen minutes

Nutrients: Caloric content: 180 Amino content: 4g Carb content: 18g Fiber content: 7g Glucose content: 5g Fatty acid: 12g

31. Alkaline Stuffed Bell Peppers

Ingredients:

- four bell peppers, any color

- one cupful cooked quinoa

- one can (1four oz) black beans, drained and rinsed

- one cupful corn kernels (fresh, frozen, or canned)

- one cupful diced tomatoes

- one-fourth cupful red onion, diced

- one-fourth cupful fresh cilantro, chopped

- one teaspoonful cumin

- half teaspoonful chili powder

- Salt and pepper to taste

Instructions:

1. Have a 375F (190C) oven ready.
2. Remove the stems and seeds from the bell peppers.
3. Put the peppers on a dish and put it in the oven.

4. Cooked quinoa, black beans, corn, diced tomatoes, red onion, cilantro, cumin, chilli powder, salt and pepper should all be combined in a big bowl.

5. Fill the quinoa mixture inside the bell peppers.

6. Bake the dish for 30–35 minutes with the foil on top.

7. Bell peppers packed with alkaline ingredients, please.

Duration: forty five minutes

Nutrients: Caloric content: 3twenty Amino content: 12g Carb content: 63g Fiber content: 14g Glucose content: 8g Fatty acid: 3g

32. Alkaline Baked Portobello Mushrooms with Spinach and Quinoa

Ingredients:

- four large portobello mushrooms

- one cupful cooked quinoa

- two cupful fresh spinach

- one-fourth cupful diced tomatoes

- two cloves garlic, minced

- one-fourth cupful fresh basil leaves, chopped

- one tablespoonful olive oil

- Salt and pepper to taste

Instructions:

1. Have a 375F (190C) oven ready.
2. The portobello mushrooms should have their stems and gills cut off.
3. Place the mushrooms, cap side up, in a baking dish.
4. Olive oil should be heated over medium heat in a skillet.
5. Cook the garlic in the oil for a full minute.
6. Fresh spinach should be stirred in and wilted.
7. Mix the cooked quinoa with the sautéed spinach, tomato cubes, basil, and the rest of the ingredients.
8. Place the quinoa stuffing in the centre of each portobello mushroom cap.

9. Use salt and pepper to taste.

10. Cook for 25–30 minutes with the foil covering the dish.

Duration: 40 minutes

Nutrients: Caloric content: 280 Amino content: 9g Carb content: 48g Fiber content: 7g Glucose content: 4g Fatty acid: 7g

33. Alkaline Roasted Vegetable Medley

Ingredients:

- two cupful broccoli florets

- two cupful cauliflower florets

- two cupful sweet potatoes, diced

- one red onion, sliced

- one red bell pepper, sliced

- one yellow bell pepper, sliced

- two tablespoonful olive oil

- one teaspoonful dried oregano

- half teaspoonful garlic powder

- Salt and pepper to taste

Instructions:

1. Have a 425F (220C) oven ready.

2. Combine the vegetables, spices, and seasonings (olive oil, dried oregano, garlic powder, salt, and pepper in a large bowl) for the broccoli, cauliflower, sweet potatoes, red onion, red bell pepper, and yellow bell pepper.

3. Create a single layer of veggies on a baking sheet.

4. Cook at 400°F for 25–30 minutes, turning once, until tender and caramelised.

Duration: thirty five minutes

CHAPTER 8

SNACKS AND APPETIZERS FOR VIBRANCY

34. Alkaline Hummus

Ingredients:

- one can (fifteen oz) chickpeas, drained and rinsed

- two cloves garlic

- three tbsp tahini

- Juice of one lemon

- two tbsp olive oil

- half tsp ground cumin

- Salt and pepper to taste

- Water as needed

Instructions:

1. In a food processor, mash together chickpeas, garlic, tahini, lemon juice, olive oil, and cumin.
2. You may adjust the consistency by adding water and blending again.
3. Taste and adjust salt and pepper.

Duration: ten minutes

Nutritional Information (per serving, about two tablespoonful):

- Caloric content: 70
- Amino content: 2g
- Carb content: 6g
- Fatty acid: 4.5g

35. Alkaline Cucumber Slices with Dill

Ingredients:

- two cucumbers
- half cupful dairy-free yogurt
- two tsp fresh dill, chopped
- Salt and pepper to taste

Instructions:

1. Cucumbers should be sliced into paper-thin circles.
2. Combine dill and yoghurt in a bowl.
3. Cover each cucumber slice with the yoghurt sauce.
4. Use salt and pepper to taste.

Duration: ten minutes

Nutritional Information (per serving, about four slices):

- Caloric content: 30
- Amino content: 1g
- Carb content: 5g

- Fatty acid: 1g

36. Alkaline Stuffed Avocado

Ingredients:

- two ripe avocados

- one cupful cherry tomatoes, halved

- half cupful red onion, finely chopped

- two tbsp balsamic vinegar

- Fresh basil leaves

- Salt and pepper to taste

Instructions:

1. Remove the pit from one avocado and cut it in half.
2. Make a well by removing some meat from each halves.
3. Cherry tomatoes, red onion, balsamic vinegar, basil, salt, and pepper should be mixed together in a bowl.
4. Spread the mixture on the avocado halves.

Duration: fifteen minutes

Nutritional Information (per serving, one avocado half):

- Caloric content: 180

- Amino content: 2g

- Carb content: 10g

- Fatty acid: 16g

37. Alkaline Zucchini Noodles with Pesto

Ingredients:

- two zucchinis, spiralized into noodles

- one cupful fresh basil leaves

- one-fourth cupful pine nuts

- two cloves garlic

- one-fourth cupful olive oil

- Juice of one lemon

- Salt and pepper to taste

Instructions:

1. Put the basil leaves, pine nuts, garlic, olive oil, and lemon juice in a blender or food processor and pulse until smooth.
2. Add water as required and blend until completely smooth.
3. Mix pesto and seasonings (salt and pepper) with zucchini noodles.

Duration: ten minutes (no cooking required for noodles)

Nutritional Information (per serving):

- Caloric content: 250

- Amino content: 4g

- Carb content: 10g

- Fatty acid: 24g

38. Alkaline Stuffed Bell Peppers

Ingredients:

- four large bell peppers (red, yellow, or green)

- one cupful quinoa

- one can black beans, drained and rinsed

- one cupful corn (fresh or frozen)

- one tsp cumin

- Salt and pepper to taste

Instructions:

1. Prepare quinoa as directed on the box.

2. Combine the quinoa, black beans, corn, cumin, salt and pepper in a bowl once it has been cooked.

3. Remove the stems and seeds from the bell peppers.

4. Fill the peppers with the quinoa stuffing.

5. Bake for 25-30 minutes at 350 degrees Fahrenheit (175 degrees Celsius).

Duration: Twenty Five-thirty minutes

Nutritional Information (per serving, one stuffed pepper):

- Caloric content: 280

- Amino content: 10g

- Carb content: 54g

- Fatty acid: 2g

39. Alkaline Baked Sweet Potato Fries

Ingredients:

- two large sweet potatoes, cut into fries

- two tbsp olive oil

- one tsp paprika

- half tsp garlic powder

- Salt and pepper to taste

Instructions:

1. Sprinkle sweet potato fries with paprika, garlic powder, salt, and pepper, then toss in olive oil.

2. Then, place them on a baking sheet in a single layer.

3. Crispy baking takes around 25 minutes at 425 degrees Fahrenheit (220 degrees Celsius).

Duration: Twenty Five-thirty minutes

Nutritional Information (per serving):

- Caloric content: 160

- Amino content: 2g

- Carb content: 30g

- Fatty acid: 4g

40. Alkaline Roasted Almonds

Ingredients:

- two cupful raw almonds

- one tbsp olive oil

- one tsp sea salt

- half tsp cayenne pepper (adjust to taste)

Instructions:

1. Combine almonds, olive oil, salt, and pepper in a bowl and toss to coat.
2. Roast at 350 degrees Fahrenheit (175 degrees Celsius) for 10 to 15 minutes, stirring periodically.

Duration: ten-fifteen minutes

Nutritional Information (per serving, about one-fourth cupful):

- Caloric content: 200

- Amino content: 6g

- Carb content: 7g

- Fatty acid: 17g

41. Alkaline Spinach and Artichoke Dip

Ingredients:

- one cupful spinach, chopped

- one cupful canned artichoke hearts, drained and chopped

- one cupful dairy-free cream cheese

- one-fourth cupful nutritional yeast

- two cloves garlic, minced

- Salt and pepper to taste

Instructions:

1. Combine everything in a bowl and stir.
2. Place in a baking dish and bake for 25 minutes at 350°F (175°C), or until bubbling and golden.

Duration: twenty-Twenty Five minutes

Nutritional Information (per serving, about one-fourth cupful):

- Caloric content: 90

- Amino content: 3g

- Carb content: 5g

- Fatty acid: 6g

42. Alkaline Mango Salsa

Ingredients:

- two ripe mangoes, diced

- half red onion, finely chopped

- one red bell pepper, diced

- one-fourth cupful fresh cilantro, chopped

- Juice of one lime

- Salt and pepper to taste

Instructions:

1. Combine all ingredients in a bowl and mix well.

Duration: fifteen minutes

Nutritional Information (per serving, about half cupful):

- Caloric content: 80

- Amino content: 1g

- Carb content: 20g

- Fatty acid: 0g

43. Alkaline Raw Veggie Platter with Almond Butter

Ingredients:

- An assortment of raw vegetables (e.g., carrots, cucumber, bell peppers, celery)

- half cupful almond butter

- one tbsp lemon juice

- Salt and pepper to taste

Instructions:

1. Vegetables should be washed and then sliced into sticks.
2. In a little bowl, combine almond butter, lemon juice, salt, and pepper.
3. Prepare an almond butter dip, and use it to serve the veggies.

Duration: No cooking required

Nutritional Information (per serving, with two tbsp of almond butter dip):

- Caloric content: 180

- Amino content: 5g

- Carb content: 10g

- Fatty acid: 14g

44. Alkaline Stuffed Mushrooms

Ingredients:

- 1two large mushrooms

- one cupful spinach, chopped

- half cupful almond meal

- two cloves garlic, minced

- one-fourth cupful nutritional yeast

- one tsp olive oil

- Salt and pepper to taste

Instructions:

1. The mushrooms should have their stems removed before being chopped.
2. Mushroom stems, spinach, and garlic should be sautéed in olive oil until softened and the flavours melded.
3. Almond meal, nutritional yeast, salt, and pepper should be added to the sautéed mixture in a bowl.
4. Put the mixture into the mushroom caps.
5. Bake for 25 minutes at 350 degrees Fahrenheit (175 degrees Celsius).

Duration: twenty-Twenty Five minutes

Nutritional Information (per serving, about three stuffed mushrooms):

- Caloric content: 80

- Amino content: 5g

- Carb content: 7g

- Fatty acid: 4g

45. Alkaline Cabbage Rolls

Ingredients:

- 8 large cabbage leaves

- one cupful quinoa, cooked

- one cupful lentils, cooked

- half cupful carrots, grated

- half cupful zucchini, grated

- half cupful tomato sauce (no sugar added)

- one tsp Italian seasoning

- Salt and pepper to taste

Instructions:

1. Remove the toughness from cabbage leaves by blanching them in boiling water for a few minutes. Drain and put away.
2. Add tomato sauce, Italian seasoning, salt and pepper to cooked quinoa and lentils, as well as grated carrots and zucchini, in a bowl and mix well.
3. Spread some of the filling down the middle of each cabbage leaf and wrap the leaves up around the filling.
4. Bake for 25 minutes at 350 degrees Fahrenheit (175 degrees Celsius).

Duration: twenty-Twenty Five minutes

Nutritional Information (per serving, two cabbage rolls):

- Caloric content: 250

- Amino content: 11g

- Carb content: 45g

- Fatty acid: 2g

46. Alkaline Watermelon and Mint Salad

Ingredients:

- four cupful watermelon, cubed

- one-fourth cupful fresh mint leaves, chopped

- Juice of one lime

- Pinch of sea salt

Instructions:

1. Mix the watermelon and mint together.
2. Add a splash of lime juice and a dash of salt.
3. Stir gently, and serve.

Duration: No cooking required

Nutritional Information (per serving, about one cupful):

- Caloric content: 50

- Amino content: 1g

- Carb content: 13g

- Fatty acid: 0g

47. Alkaline Roasted Red Pepper and Walnut Dip

Ingredients:

- two red bell peppers

- half cupful walnuts

- two cloves garlic

- two tbsp olive oil

- Juice of one lemon

- Salt and pepper to taste

Instructions:

1. You may scorch the skin of red peppers by roasting them in the oven or over a flame. Remove the seeds and cut the peels.
2. Roasted red peppers, walnuts, garlic, olive oil, lemon juice, salt, and pepper are processed until smooth in a food processor.

Duration: twenty-Twenty Five minutes (for roasting peppers)

Nutritional Information (per serving, about two tablespoonful):

- Caloric content: 100

- Amino content: 2g

- Carb content: 3g

- Fatty acid: 9g

48. Alkaline Carrot and Ginger Soup

Ingredients:

- four cupful carrots, chopped

- one small onion, chopped

- two inches fresh ginger, minced

- four cupful vegetable broth

- one tsp turmeric

- Salt and pepper to taste

Instructions:

1. Onions and ginger should be sautéed until aromatic in a saucepan.
2. Cooking with turmeric, vegetable broth, and diced carrots.
3. Keep cooking until carrots are fork-tender.
4. Whisk together to the point of smoothness.
5. Use salt and pepper to taste.

Duration: thirty minutes

Nutritional Information (per serving, about one cupful):

- Caloric content: 60

- Amino content: 1g

- Carb content: 14g

- Fatty acid: 0g

49. Alkaline Chia Seed Pudding

Ingredients:

- three tbsp chia seeds

- one cupful almond milk

- half tsp vanilla extract

- half cupful fresh berries (e.g., blueberries, strawberries)

- one tbsp sliced almonds

Instructions:

1. To make chia seed vanilla almond milk, combine the ingredients in a glass container.
2. Allow to thicken in the fridge for at least four hours, preferably overnight.
3. Serve with sliced almonds and fresh berries on top.

Duration: four hours (for setting)

Nutritional Information (per serving):

- Caloric content: 200

- Amino content: 5g

- Carb content: 16g

- Fatty acid: 11g

50. Alkaline Stuffed Tomatoes

Ingredients:

- four large tomatoes

- one cupful cooked quinoa

- half cupful black olives, chopped

- half cupful cucumber, diced

- one-fourth cupful red onion, finely chopped

- Fresh basil leaves

- Salt and pepper to taste

Instructions:

1. Tomatoes may be used by cutting off the tops and scooping out the pulp.
2. Combine the quinoa, olives, onions, cucumber, salt, and pepper in a bowl.
3. Put the mixture into the tomatoes.
4. Use fresh basil leaves as a garnish.

Duration: fifteen minutes

Nutritional Information (per serving, one stuffed tomato):

- Caloric content: 180

- Amino content: 4g

- Carb content: 30g

- Fatty acid: 5g

CHAPTER 9

DESSERTS AND SWEET TREATS, THE ALKALINE WAY

51. Alkaline Chia Seed Pudding

Ingredients:

- three tbsp chia seeds

- one cupful almond milk

- half tsp vanilla extract

- half cupful fresh berries (e.g., blueberries, strawberries)

- one tbsp sliced almonds

Instructions:

1. To make chia seed vanilla almond milk, combine the ingredients in a glass container.
2. Allow to thicken in the fridge for at least four hours, preferably overnight.
3. Serve with sliced almonds and fresh berries on top.

Duration: four hours (for setting)

Nutritional Information (per serving):

- Caloric content: 200

- Amino content: 5g

- Carb content: 16g

- Fatty acid: 11g

52. Alkaline Avocado Chocolate Mousse

Ingredients:

- two ripe avocados

- one-fourth cupful unsweetened cocoa powder

- one-fourth cupful almond milk

- one-fourth cupful maple syrup or agave nectar

- one tsp vanilla extract

- Pinch of salt

Instructions:

1. Put everything in a blender or food processor and blitz until smooth.
2. Put in the fridge and let it chill for at least two hours.

Duration: two hours (for chilling)

Nutritional Information (per serving):

- Caloric content: 220

- Amino content: 3g

- Carb content: 21g

- Fatty acid: 16g

53. Alkaline Banana Ice Cream

Ingredients:

- four ripe bananas, sliced and frozen

- one tsp vanilla extract

- two tbsp almond milk

Instructions:

1. Throw some frozen banana slices into the blender.
2. Blend with some almond milk and vanilla essence.
3. Mix it up until it's nice and creamy.
4. Start serving right now.

Duration: five minutes

Nutritional Information (per serving):

- Caloric content: 110

- Amino content: 1g

- Carb content: 29g

- Fatty acid: 0g

54. Alkaline Berry Sorbet

Ingredients:

- two cupful mixed berries (e.g., strawberries, blueberries, raspberries)

- one tbsp lemon juice

- two tbsp maple syrup or agave nectar

Instructions:

1. In a blender, combine the berries, lemon juice, and sugar.
2. Put in an airtight container and freeze for two hours.
3. Simply scoop and serve.

Duration: two hours (for freezing)

Nutritional Information (per serving):

- Caloric content: 70
- Amino content: 1g
- Carb content: 17g
- Fatty acid: 0g

55. Alkaline Date and Nut Energy Balls

Ingredients:

- one cupful dates, pitted
- one cupful mixed nuts (e.g., almonds, walnuts)
- two tbsp chia seeds
- two tbsp unsweetened cocoa powder
- one tsp vanilla extract
- Pinch of salt
- Unsweetened shredded coconut for rolling

Instructions:

1. Combine the salt, vanilla extract, salt, dates, nuts, chia seeds, cocoa powder, and salt in a food processor.
2. Combine and knead until the dough is sticky.
3. Compact into tiny balls.
4. Shredded coconut may be used as a coating for the balls.
5. Put in the fridge and chill for 30 minutes before serving.

Duration: thirty minutes (for chilling)

Nutritional Information (per serving, about two balls):

- Caloric content: 180

- Amino content: 4g

- Carb content: 24g

- Fatty acid: 9g

56. Alkaline Baked Apple with Cinnamon

Ingredients:

- two apples

- one tsp cinnamon

- one tbsp coconut oil

- two tbsp chopped nuts (e.g., almonds, walnuts)

- one tbsp maple syrup

Instructions:

1. Turn on the oven to 350 degrees Fahrenheit (175 degrees Celsius).
2. Put the apples in a baking dish and core them.
3. Combine maple syrup, chopped almonds, coconut oil, and cinnamon.
4. Put the filling in the apples.
5. Cook for 25–30 minutes, or until apples are soft.

Duration: Twenty Five-thirty minutes

Nutritional Information (per serving):

- Caloric content: 200

- Amino content: 2g

- Carb content: 30g

- Fatty acid: 9g

57. Alkaline Lemon Poppy Seed Muffins

Ingredients:

- two cupful almond flour

- one-fourth cupful coconut flour

- one-fourth cupful poppy seeds

- one tsp baking soda

- Pinch of salt

- Zest and juice of two lemons

- 3/four cupful unsweetened applesauce

- one-fourth cupful maple syrup or agave nectar

- three eggs

Instructions:

1. Turn on the oven to 350 degrees Fahrenheit (175 degrees Celsius).
2. Put the flours, poppy seeds, baking soda, and salt into a bowl with the almond flour and coconut flour.
3. Mix the eggs, applesauce, maple syrup, and lemon zest in a separate basin.
4. Combine the liquid and dry ingredients in a large mixing bowl.
5. Fill muffin cups with the batter.
6. Bake until a toothpick inserted in the centre comes out clean, about 25 minutes.

Duration: twenty-Twenty Five minutes

Nutritional Information (per muffin):

- Caloric content: 160

- Amino content: 6g

- Carb content: 14g

- Fatty acid: 9g

58. Alkaline Chocolate-Dipped Strawberries

Ingredients:

- one cupful strawberries

- one-fourth cupful dark chocolate (70% cocoa or higher)

- one tsp coconut oil

Instructions:

1. Dark chocolate and coconut oil should be melted together in a double boiler or the microwave.
2. Melt some chocolate and dip each strawberry into it.
3. Put on a tray lined with parchment paper, then chill in the fridge to set the chocolate.

Duration: ten minutes (for chilling)

Nutritional Information (per serving, about four strawberries):

- Caloric content: 90

- Amino content: 1g

- Carb content: 8g

- Fatty acid: 6g

59. Alkaline Papaya Sorbet

Ingredients:

- one ripe papaya, peeled, seeded, and cubed

- one lime, juiced

- two tbsp maple syrup or agave nectar

- Mint leaves for garnish

Instructions:

1. Blend or process the papaya cubes, lime juice, and sugar until smooth.
2. Whisk together to the point of smoothness.
3. Put in the freezer for two hours.

4. Divide into dishes and top with fresh mint.

Duration: two hours (for freezing)

Nutritional Information (per serving):

- Caloric content: 120

- Amino content: 1g

- Carb content: 30g

- Fatty acid: 0g

60. Alkaline Mixed Fruit Salad with Lime-Mint Dressing

Ingredients:

- two cupful mixed fruits (e.g., pineapple, mango, kiwi)

- Juice of one lime

- one tbsp maple syrup or agave nectar

- Fresh mint leaves for garnish

Instructions:

1. Put the chopped mixed fruits in a basin.
2. Lime juice and sugar may be combined in a separate dish.
3. Dress the fruit salad and sprinkle with mint for a fresh finish.

Duration: No cooking required

Nutritional Information (per serving, about one cupful):

- Caloric content: 70

- Amino content: 1g

- Carb content: 18g

- Fatty acid: 0g

61. Alkaline Almond and Coconut Energy Bars

Ingredients:

- one cupful almonds

- half cupful shredded coconut

- half cupful pitted dates

- one-fourth cupful almond butter

- one-fourth cupful water

- half tsp vanilla extract

- Pinch of salt

Instructions:

1. Combine almonds, coconut, and dates in a food processor.
2. Combine until a crumbly texture is achieved.
3. Put in some almond butter, water, vanilla, salt, and salt.
4. Combine and process until a dough is formed.
5. Put the mixture in a baking dish that has been coated with foil and chill it for at least an hour.
6. Form into bars.

Duration: one hour (for chilling)

Nutritional Information (per serving, one bar):

- Caloric content: 180

- Amino content: 4g

- Carb content: 17g

- Fatty acid: 12g

62. Alkaline Blueberry Oatmeal Cookies

Ingredients:

- one cupful rolled oats

- half cupful almond flour

- half cupful blueberries (fresh or frozen)

- one-fourth cupful maple syrup or agave nectar

- one-fourth cupful coconut oil

- one tsp vanilla extract

- half tsp baking powder

- Pinch of salt

Instructions:

1. Turn on the oven to 350 degrees Fahrenheit (175 degrees Celsius).
2. To make these, mix together some rolled oats, almond flour, blueberries, maple syrup, coconut oil, vanilla extract, baking powder, and salt in a bowl.
3. To ensure a successful blend, mix well.
4. Spoon the dough onto a baking sheet.
5. Spread the cookie dough out with a fork.
6. Put it in the oven for 15–20 minutes, or until the top is brown.

Duration: fifteen twenty minutes

Nutritional Information (per cookie):

- Caloric content: 110

- Amino content: 2g

- Carb content: 13g

- Fatty acid: 6g

63. Alkaline Raw Nut and Date Bars

Ingredients:

- one cupful mixed nuts (e.g., almonds, walnuts)

- one cupful pitted dates

- one-fourth cupful unsweetened shredded coconut

- one-fourth cupful chia seeds

- one-fourth cupful almond butter

- one tsp vanilla extract

- Pinch of salt

Instructions:

1. Put a variety of nuts, dates, coconut, chia seeds, almond butter, vanilla, and salt into a food processor and pulse until combined.
2. Mix well until a sticky dough forms.
3. Put the mixture in a baking dish that has been coated with foil and chill it for at least an hour.
4. Form into bars.

Duration: one hour (for chilling)

Nutritional Information (per serving, one bar):

- Caloric content: 180

- Amino content: 4g

- Carb content: 18g

- Fatty acid: 10g

64. Alkaline Mango and Coconut Sorbet

Ingredients:

- two ripe mangoes, peeled and cubed

- one-fourth cupful shredded coconut

- Juice of one lime

- two tbsp maple syrup or agave nectar

Instructions:

1. Blend or process mango pieces, shredded coconut, lime juice, and sweetener until smooth.
2. Whisk together to the point of smoothness.
3. Put in the freezer for two hours.
4. Put servings in dishes using a scoop.

Duration: two hours (for freezing)

Nutritional Information (per serving):

- Caloric content: 140

- Amino content: 1g

- Carb content: 35g

- Fatty acid: 1g

65. Alkaline Cinnamon and Almond Baked Apples

Ingredients:

- four apples

- one-fourth cupful almond butter

- two tbsp chopped almonds

- one tsp cinnamon

- one-fourth cupful water

- two tbsp maple syrup or agave nectar

Instructions:

1. Turn on the oven to 350 degrees Fahrenheit (175 degrees Celsius).
2. Put the apples in a baking dish and core them.
3. Mix almond butter, almonds, cinnamon, water, and sugar in a bowl.
4. Put some of the almond filling in an apple.
5. Wait 25 minutes to see whether the apples are done.

Duration: twenty-Twenty Five minutes

Nutritional Information (per serving):

- Caloric content: 180

- Amino content: 3g

- Carb content: 25g

- Fatty acid: 9g

66. Alkaline Almond and Apricot Energy Bites

Ingredients:

- one cupful almonds

- half cupful dried apricots

- one-fourth cupful unsweetened shredded coconut

- one-fourth cupful almond butter

- one tsp vanilla extract

- Pinch of salt

Instructions:

1. Process almonds, dried apricots, coconut, almond butter, vanilla essence, and salt in a food processor until well combined.
2. Mix well until a sticky dough forms.
3. Compact bites of energy may be made from the combination.
4. Make sure it chills in the fridge for at least half an hour before serving.

Duration: thirty minutes (for chilling)

Nutritional Information (per serving, about two bites):

- Caloric content: 140

- Amino content: 3g

- Carb content: 11g

- Fatty acid: 9g

67. Alkaline Cucumber and Avocado Salsa

Ingredients:

- two cucumbers, diced

- two ripe avocados, diced

- one-fourth red onion, finely chopped

- one-fourth cupful fresh cilantro, chopped

- Juice of two limes

- Salt and pepper to taste

Instructions:

1. In a bowl, combine the diced cucumbers, avocados, red onion, and fresh cilantro.

2. Squeeze the lime juice over the mixture.

3. Season with salt and pepper.

4. Toss gently to combine.

5. Serve your alkaline cucumber and avocado salsa with whole-grain tortilla chips or vegetable sticks.

Duration: ten minutes

Nutrients: Caloric content: 140 Amino content: 2g Carb content: 11g Fiber content: 6g Glucose content: 2g Fatty acid: 11g

68. Alkaline Sweet Potato Hummus

Ingredients:

- two cupful sweet potatoes, diced and roasted

- one can (fifteen oz) chickpeas, drained and rinsed

- two cloves garlic

- two tablespoonful tahini

- Juice of one lemon

- two tablespoonful olive oil

- half teaspoonful ground cumin

- Salt and pepper to taste

Instructions:

1. In a food processor, combine the roasted sweet potatoes, chickpeas, garlic, tahini, lemon juice, olive oil, ground cumin, salt, and pepper.

2. Blend until smooth and creamy.

3. Serve your alkaline sweet potato hummus with vegetable sticks or whole-grain crackers.

Duration: twenty minutes

Nutrients: Caloric content: 160 Amino content: 4g Carb content: 22g Fiber content: 6g Glucose content: 3g Fatty acid: 7g

69. Alkaline Date and Walnut Bars

Ingredients:

- one cupful dates, pitted and soaked in warm water for ten minutes

- one cupful walnuts

- half cupful shredded coconut

- one-fourth cupful cacao powder

- half tsp vanilla extract

- A pinch of sea salt

Instructions:

1. Drain the soaked dates.

2. Blend dates, walnuts, shredded coconut, cacao powder, vanilla extract, and sea salt until the mixture holds together.

3. Press the mixture into a square baking dish and refrigerate for thirty minutes.

4. Cut into bars and serve.

Duration: thirty minutes (for chilling)

Nutritional Information (per serving, one bar):

- Caloric content: 180

- Amino content: 3g

- Carb content: 16g

- Fatty acid: 12g

70. Alkaline Fruit Salad with Mint

Ingredients:

- two cupful mixed fruits (e.g., melon, kiwi, berries)

- Fresh mint leaves

- Juice of one lime

Instructions:

1. Cut mixed fruits into bite-sized pieces and place them in a bowl.

2. Squeeze lime juice over the fruit and garnish with fresh mint leaves.

Duration: No cooking required

Nutritional Information (per serving, about one cupful):

- Caloric content: 60

- Amino content: 1g

- Carb content: 15g

- Fatty acid: 0g

CONCLUSION

In conclusion, the Alkaline Nutrition Cookbook is not just a collection of recipes; it's a guide to a vibrant and healthier way of living. Throughout this book, you've embarked on a journey to discover the benefits of alkaline nutrition, explored the fascinating history and scientific principles behind it, and learned how to make better dietary choices for your well-being. You've gained insights into the body's pH balance, the role of alkaline minerals, and the potential for reducing the risk of chronic diseases through mindful eating.

You've also acquired the knowledge and skills needed to assess your current diet, transition to an alkaline lifestyle, and optimize your meal planning and food choices. We've provided you with a wide array of delicious and satisfying recipes for breakfast, lunch, dinner, and snacks, all designed to nourish your body, improve your digestion, boost your immunity. By understanding food labels, choosing organic and seasonal produce, and being mindful of budget-friendly shopping and food storage, you've empowered yourself to make informed choices that support your health while being considerate of the environment.

We encourage you to explore, experiment, and enjoy the recipes in this cookbook, and to share the knowledge you've gained with friends and family. Alkaline nutrition is not just a diet; it's a lifestyle, and as you embrace it, you're taking a significant step toward living a life of balance, health, and vibrancy.

Thank you for joining us on this journey, and we wish you many years of delicious, nutritious, and alkaline eating. May your path be filled with good health and boundless energy.

Printed in Great Britain
by Amazon